ARABIC   ASTRONOMY   BANKING   BEE-KEEPING   BIOLOGY
ANISATION   CALCULUS   CHEMISTRY
OMMERCIAL CORRESPON   NG   TO
KING   CRICKET   DRAW   DUTTON
ELECTRICITY IN THE   MBROIDERY
ENGLISH RENASCENCE   ROMANTIC
EVERYDAY FRENCH   T   TO FLY
E BOOK   GARDENING   RAPHY OF
ONARY   GERMAN GRA   GERMAN PHRASE BOOK   GOLF
GOOD FARM ACCOUNTING   GOOD FARM CROPS   GOOD FARMING
T FARMING   GOOD GRASSLAND   GOOD AND HEALTHY ANIMALS
GOOD POULTRY KEEPING   GOOD SHEEP FARMING   GOOD SOIL
E   HINDUSTANI   HISTORY: ABRAHAM LINCOLN ALEXANDER THE
U   CONSTANTINE   COOK   CRANMER   ERASMUS   GLADSTONE AND
ILTON   PERICLES   PETER THE GREAT   PUSHKIN   RALEIGH   RICHELIEU
DROW   EMENT
IAN   LETTER
ENGIN   ···· AND HE WILL BE   ANICS
DERN   ORING
HILOSO   YET WISER Proverbs 9.9   HYSICS
LUMBI   PUBLIC
ECKO   USSIAN
ITS N   AND PURPOSE   SOCCER   SPANISH   SPE   AND
SWA   SWEDISH   TEACHING   THINKING   TRIG   METRY
BRIT H RAILWAYS FOR BOYS   CAMPING FOR BOYS AND GIRLS
OR GIRLS   MODELMAKING FOR BOYS   NEEDLEWORK FOR GIRLS
OYS AND GIRLS   SAILING AND SMALL BOATS FOR BOYS AND GIRLS
RK FOR BOYS   ADVERTISING & PUBLICITY   ALGEBRA   AMATEUR
NG   BIOLOGY   BOOK-KEEPING   BRICKWORK   BRINGING UP
TRY   CHEMISTRY   CHESS   CHINESE   COMMERCIAL ARITHMETIC
RAVELLING   TO COMPOSE MUSIC   CONSTRUCTIONAL DETAILS
G   DUTCH   DUTTON SPEEDWORDS   ECONOMIC GEOGRAPHY
T   EMBROIDERY   ENGLISH GRAMMAR   LITERARY APPRECIATION
AL   ROMANTIC REVIVAL   VICTORIAN AGE   CONTEMPORARY
FISHING   TO FLY   FREELANCE WRITING   FRENCH   FRENCH
USE   GEOGRAPHY OF LIVING THINGS   GEOLOGY   GEOMETRY
SE BOOK   GOLF   GOOD CONTROL OF INSECT PESTS   GOOD
ARM CROPS   GOOD FARMING   GOOD FARMING BY MACHINE
D   GOOD AND HEALTHY ANIMALS   GOOD MARKET GARDENING
GOOD SHEEP FARMING   GOOD SOIL   GOOD ENGLISH   GREEK
RY: ABRAHAM LINCOLN   ALEXANDER THE GREAT   BOLIVAR   BOTHA
ANMER   ERASMUS   GLADSTONE AND LIBERALISM   HENRY V   JOAN OF
T PUSHKIN   RALEIGH   RICHELIEU   ROBESPIERRE   THOMAS JEFFERSON
OME NURSING   HORSE MANAGEMENT   HOUSEHOLD DOCTOR
RNALISM   LATIN   LAWN TENNIS   LETTER WRITER   MALAY
ONENTS   WORKSHOP PRACTICE   MECHANICS   MECHANICAL
MORE GERMAN   MOTHERCRAFT   MOTORING   MOTOR CYCLING
HY   PHYSICAL GEOGRAPHY   PHYSICS   PHYSIOLOGY   PITMAN'S
ESE   PSYCHOLOGY   PUBLIC ADMINISTRATION   PUBLIC SPEAKING

THE TEACH YOURSELF BOOKS
EDITED BY LEONARD CUTTS

RUGBY FOOTBALL

THE TEACH YOURSELF BOOKS

RUGBY FOOTBALL

By

F. N. S. CREEK

M.B.E., M.C. B.A.

THE ENGLISH UNIVERSITIES PRESS LTD

102 NEWGATE STREET

LONDON, E.C.I

First Printed 1950
Reprinted 1956
New and improved impression 1959

Printed in Great Britain for the English Universities Press, Limited,
by Richard Clay and Company, Ltd., Bungay, Suffolk

CONTENTS

CHAP.   PAGE

I. How to Start 9

II. A Short History of the Game . . 17

III. The Laws of Rugby Football . . 22

IV. Basic Principles 62

V. Useful Practices 85

VI. Forward Play 110

VII. Outside Play 140

VIII. The Control of the Game . . 187

IX. Modern Tendencies 194

LIST OF PLATES

A Harlequin player tries to fall on the ball as P. W. Kininmonth (Richmond and Scotland) leads a forward dribble.

T. Allan (Wallabies) shows good form in a dive over the London Counties' line to score a try.

Lt. J. Matthews (Army and Wales) goes for the Navy line with great resolution.

Three Harlequin forwards well to the fore in a line-out against Richmond.

A scrum-half throws out a long pass.

R. Uren, England's full-back, shows the moment of impact as he attempts to convert a try against Scotland.

A later stage of another conversion—a good high kick.

An England stand-off half about to start a three-quarter movement against Wales.

An early stage in the formation of a loose scrum.

A. F. Dorward (Cambridge and Scotland) gets the ball out to Glyn Davies (Cambridge and Wales) from a scrum on the half-way line.

(*Between pages* 96 *and* 97.)

ACKNOWLEDGMENTS

The author and publishers acknowledge with thanks permission to reproduce the photographs appearing in this book, which were supplied by *The Sport and General Press Agency*.

The Laws given in Chapter III, and Notes for the Guidance of Referees in Chapter VIII, are included by permission of the *Rugby Football Union*.

CHAPTER I

HOW TO START

THE purpose of this book, like that of the others in this series, is to provide the ordinary person with so much knowledge of the Game of Rugby football that he can literally teach himself how to play, always bearing in mind the fact that he is dependent on twenty-nine other players. An acquaintance with the principles of the game, its laws, and some of the main tactical points is obviously invaluable to the player before he ever sets foot on a pitch. Equally important is enthusiasm for the game, for Rugger is not a sport which can be played half-heartedly. There can be no surer way of awakening such enthusiasm than by going to a first-class match, an international for preference.

For Rugger enthusiasts all over the world—and certainly for the English—the name of Twickenham conjures up all that is most thrilling and exhilarating in the game. Let us visit this headquarters of the Rugby game in imagination one spring afternoon and watch the annual match between England and Scotland for the Calcutta Cup, that unique trophy for which only two teams compete.

The train from Waterloo is packed with enthusiasts, mostly be-ribboned partisans with a single subject for conversation, discussing the merits of this forward and that three-quarter, criticising the selectors perhaps, but unanimous in their view that it will be a great match. The vast stands of the ground are visible from far away, and as we draw near in the long procession from Twickenham station, we can hear the murmur of the crowds already inside. Passing round the back of the east stand, we buy an official programme and emerge into the sunshine. Here, at the end of the stand, we stop for a brief moment and look around, for it is a most impressive scene. Many a spectator, arriving at Twickenham for the first time, has stared, amazed at the sight of thousands upon thousands of people banked up high in the double tiers of the vast stands. These stands form a gigantic U, surrounding the pitch on the east, west, and north sides, while at the southern end are the stone terraces where the hardier mortals stand.

Out in the middle, soon to be the focus of attention, lies a rectangle of dark-green lush grass, marked out with white lines of mathematical precision. Flags mark the four corners and the ends of the half-way and " twenty-five " lines, and these and the Union Jack on the end of the north stand are flickering animatedly in the light breeze blowing straight up the ground from the south. In the centre of the pitch a Guards band is playing a lively selection of Sullivan melodies, while round the edge of the field walks a small boy carrying a board which bears the chalk-written announcement that the

England right-wing three-quarter is not, as originally selected, the Oxford University "Blue" but
the tall, long-striding doctor from one of the London
hospitals.

We move along to our ring-side seats, almost level
with the centre line, and as we do so, the band
stops playing, makes a smart right turn, and marches
off to the small block of seats in the west stand
next to the entrance to the dressing-rooms. The
murmur of the crowd suddenly hushes; the Press
photographers station themselves in a rough semi-
circle in front of the players' entrance and crouch
or poise expectantly. There is a sudden yell and a
storm of hand-clapping as Scotland's captain trots
out on to the pitch, leading his team in their blue
shirts and white shorts. The cheering dies away,
only to swell out louder than ever as the stands
thunder their welcome to the England team, whose
white shirts and shorts dazzle with what can be
only a temporary cleanness. Behind them comes
the referee in a distinctive faded red jersey and
blue shorts. The toss having taken place in the
dressing-room, we now see that England, defending
the half to our right, are playing against the breeze.
The England stand-off half places the ball for the
kick-off, the referee looks at his watch and at the
two captains, who signal readiness, the whistle
sounds, and the game has begun.

The kick is long and low, towards the east touch-
line. A tall second-row forward catches it for Scotland and pivots on his left foot to kick for touch.

But he is too slow, for three England forwards are up with the ball and overwhelm him. Both packs gather round and shove for possession; Scotland heel, their scrum-half picks up and in one rapid movement swings to his left and throws a long, fast pass out to his partner. Out goes the ball to the left centre three-quarter; he jinks to his left, moving inside his opposite number, the England right centre, but a wing forward streaks across to intercept him, brings him down with a crashing tackle, and the ball runs loose. The Scottish pack are up on it immediately, and storm over the half-way line with the ball at their feet; it is an inspiring sight as that wave of blue shirts sweeps onward. The England full-back runs crouching to meet the on-coming rush; he throws himself at the feet of the forwards, his back towards them, and gathers the ball in with one sweep to his body. Quickly the England pack gathers round and there is a terrific mêlée. The whistle blows, and the referee orders a set scrum 2 yards outside the English twenty-five line.

The short, stocky England scrum-half puts the ball in; England heel it, and it quickly travels out to the left wing, who streaks away up the touch-line, swerves inside his opposite number, and with a long, low kick finds touch a yard inside the Scottish half. The throw-in reaches a tall second-row Scottish forward in the middle of the line-out; the ball is down; Scotland heel it, and their three-quarter line is away. The ball flashes from man to man until it reaches the left centre, and then the Scottish full-back, tearing up from behind, takes a pass at full speed, crosses the half-way line and, drawing the England right wing, passes out to the Scottish winger. Off he darts for the corner flag with only the full-back to beat. As the full-back comes across to tackle, the winger checks in his stride and swerves to the right, and the full-back, diving at his knees, misses. To the deafening cheers of Scotland's supporters, the wing swerves outward again and crashes over the line, half-way between the touch-line and the goal-posts. A perfectly orthodox movement, assisted by the speed and skill of the wing three-quarter, earns a well-merited three points.

All round the ground there is a sudden stillness. Through our binoculars we can see the full-back as he runs up to kick. The ball rises high into the air, hangs for a split second, and then glides down between the tops of the posts. There is another roar from the crowd as the two touch judges, one behind each goal-post, raise their flags, and Scotland are five points up.

Faced with this early set-back, England fight back hard, the pack especially working like terriers, gathering round any loose ball, packing low, and pushing their opponents off the ball three times out of four. But the Scottish line are magnificent in defence; they come up on the England threes every time, leaving no gaps as each man crashes his opposite number down. The English halves and centres are trying all they know to find an opening. There are short punts ahead and cross kicks from the wings, but the Scottish full-back is always in position. With the slight breeze behind him, he is kicking magnificently—long, raking kicks of 40 to 50 yards, and towering cork-screw clearances in the face of an avalanche of bustling, tireless forwards. Up to half-time the game ranges backwards and forwards, hardly and cleanly fought, neither side missing opportunities, but both tackling hard and without hesitation.

With the whistle for half-time, and Scotland still holding their five-point lead, we relax for a while as the players take an easy and suck the welcome slices of lemon. Soon after the re-start, the ball is hooked by England; it is out of the scrum and passed to the stand-off half in a flash. Without pausing, he passes straight out to the left centre, and the ball travels smartly across to the right wing. Outside him there suddenly appears the stand-off half, who has run at top speed as soon as he passed, and who now receives the ball again. For a second the defence is shaken, but the Scottish full-back and a wing forward are racing to intercept him. He pauses and kicks high and forward into the centre of the field. With the full-back drawn out of position, three England forwards tear after the ball; the captain, a second-row forward, has it, and unopposed charges 10 yards to ground it between the posts to make the score 5–3. The quick-passing movement and the cleverly placed cross kick

receive a great roar of applause from the crowd,
followed immediately by the sudden silence as the
full-back kicks at goal and a second roar as the
ball sails between the posts to make the scores
level.

Now both sides alternate with strong attacking
movements. First one pack, then the other, surges
down the field. The England scrum-half breaks
away on the blind side, but two Scottish forwards
bring him to the ground. The Scottish right centre
weaves his way through the English defence, only
to fumble his final pass to the wing. Then an English winger is in full cry down the touch-line with
the Scottish full-back racing across to intercept;
3 yards from the line he hurls winger and ball into
touch. The crowd is on its feet, yelling with excite-
ment, but an eager England forward, charging into
the Scottish line, is penalised, and from the resulting
kick the pressure is relieved. The rest of the match
is one long repetition of scrums, line-outs, scissors
movements, forward rushes, and stern defence; but
neither side can break through for that vital deciding
score before the final whistle sounds for " No-
side ".

The thousands of spectators rise quietly to their
feet as the roll of drums announces the first chords
of the National Anthem. Below on the pitch, the
players and the referee are still; flags wave gently,
and the only sound is that of the music rising and
falling on the breeze. It is all over. A wonderful
game, to be discussed as we go back to the station,

where the big crowd is marshalled with swiftness and efficiency on to the special trains for Waterloo; a game to be debated for many years to come by all who are thrilled by the beauty and skill and speed of Rugby football at its best.

CHAPTER II

A SHORT HISTORY OF THE GAME

LIKE its sister game, Association Football, modern Rugger can claim to have been descended from an ancient Roman game whose object was to kick, carry, or force a ball across a line marked on the ground in the rear of the opposing team. After the Roman occupation was ended, little is known of football, except for various statutes forbidding the game! These laws were necessary because some of the serious brawls into which most of the games degenerated resulted in many casualties. Yet the players must have been very keen, for in spite of statutes by Edward II (forbidding Londoners to " hustle over large balls "), Edward III (ordering his sheriffs to suppress the game), James I (debarring " all rough and violent exercise as the foot ball, meeter for laming than for making able the users thereof"), and Charles II (again making the game unlawful) youths still went on playing. Annual struggles took place every Shrove Tuesday in Chester and at Corfe Castle, with large numbers of players on each side, and inter-parish games were common.

Later, a certain semblance of order developed, as in the famous description of the football match at Rugby School in *Tom Brown's Schooldays*, but even then some of the onlookers joined in the fun. The next stage was in 1823, when that small boy at Rugby, William Webb Ellis, as the inscription to his memory says, " with a fine disregard for the rules of football as played in his time, first took the ball in his arms and ran with it ". That was the real birth of our modern game of Rugby football.

It should be realised that the development of Rugger has been very much dependent on the evolution of the actual ball itself. In the early days, the bladders of the footballs were pigs' bladders, so there was no standard size ball—they varied according to the size of the pig! It is said that the Rugby school boot-maker used to make the leather covers to fit these bladders and then blew them up with his own lungs; and those old balls, being rather bigger and much rounder than their modern counterparts, were better for drop-kicking and dribbling. The plum-stone-shaped ball originated when india-rubber bladders were first made, and it seems to have been chosen because it was easier to catch and carry than the round ball. Originally, too, the pieces of leather which made up the skin used to be sewn together, so that the seams looked like the lines of longitude on a school globe; but this cover was weak where they all joined, so they are now put together rather like bricks in a wall, thus making the whole outer casing very much stronger.

Except for the above-mentioned kinds of " mob " football, the game was played very little at the beginning of the nineteenth century, but after that the Public Schools began to take it up more seriously. While most of them continued with the dribbling game, which later developed into soccer, Rugby remained loyal to the handling code. Then in the early sixties a great fillip to Rugger was provided by the foundation of Blackheath and the Richmond clubs, and others soon followed. In 1871 the Rugby Union was formed, mainly at the instigation of these two clubs, and this was followed in the same year by the first international match between England and Scotland, won, incidentally, by Scotland. At the meeting in London to form the Rugby Union, the following clubs were represented : Blackheath, Richmond, Civil Service, Marlborough Nomads, West Kent, Wimbledon Hornets, Gipsies, Clapham Rovers, Law, Wellington College, Guy's Hospital, Flamingoes, Harlequins, Queen's House, King's College, St. Paul's School, Lausanne, Addison, Mohicans, and Belsize Park.

Even as recently as the seventies, Rugger was played with twenty players on each side, the usual formation at that time being three full-backs, three half-backs, and fourteen forwards. No wonder that the tight scrums often lasted for five or ten minutes on end! The year 1875 was an important one, for in that season's Varsity match the number of players was reduced from twenty to fifteen aside, and " tries " decided the results of matches if an equal number of goals had been scored. Gradually the game became more open as, one after another, players were withdrawn from the "pack" to increase the scoring power of the "outsides". The Dominions and other countries took up the game, tours became popular, scoring was very similar to what it is now-a-days, and the stage was set for the steady evolution of Rugger to the position it has attained to-day.

The method of scoring has gone through many changes since the early days. Up to 1875 matches were decided by goals only, but after that tries were introduced. Later, in 1887, the system of scoring by "points" was adopted, a try being counted as one point, and a goal as three points. Two years later the "penalty goal", worth two points, was introduced. Then, at intervals, the try and the penalty goal were increased to three points, and a marked goal was reduced to three. Finally, after much controversy, the value of a dropped goal was in 1948 reduced from four to three points.

The Rugby Football Union is the parent body with headquarters at Twickenham; its object is the furtherance of the interests of the game, and it is in membership with the International Rugby Football Board, a body composed of two representatives of each of the four Home Unions and one representative from each of the Unions of Australia, New Zealand, and South Africa. One of the duties of this Board is to frame, interpret, and make any necessary alterations in the Laws of the Game. The amateur status of the game is very strictly preserved, and the Board has passed resolutions to the effect that the employment of a paid trainer or coach is contrary to the principles of amateur Rugger, and that no memento exceeding the value of £5 shall be given to players. This jealously guarded amateurism has led to a complete break-away by Rugby League or Northern Union enthusiasts ; this variation of Rugger is played by thirteen aside, but it is beyond the scope of this book.

CHAPTER III

THE LAWS OF RUGBY FOOTBALL

IF the reader of this book is really determined to teach himself something about the game of Rugby football, it is essential for him to give some serious consideration to the printed laws. It would be an interesting test to take the thirty players before an ordinary Saturday-afternoon club match and inquire how many of them could honestly say that they had read completely through the laws of the game which they were about to play; the percentage of delinquents would probably be quite surprising. Learning by one's own mistakes on the field of play is a typically British weakness; we wrongly imagine it to be the correct, light-hearted approach to what is, after all, merely a game. Yet—to take one only simple example—Rugger is a tough game, and if its players do not know the elementary rules, it can quite easily degenerate into a highly dangerous game. The keen beginner, therefore, will do his best to learn the laws and their application by reading carefully through this chapter in the hope that he will not commit any " howlers " when he takes the field in his first important match.

The Laws of Rugby Football are subdivided into four parts. Law 1 is merely a plan of the field;

Law 2 consists of definitions and a glossary of terms; Laws 3 to 11 are concerned with the preliminaries to a game—ground, ball, dress, scoring, referee, and touch-judges; and Laws 12 to 37 deal with the actual play in detail. In addition to these rather prosaic laws, the Rugby Football Union issues a series of notes for the guidance of referees; and since much can be learned from these notes, they will be incorporated in this chapter in any explanations which are considered necessary after each law has been quoted in full. Here they are, then, commencing with

LAW I.   PLAN OF THE FIELD

The Plan, including all words and figures thereon, is to take effect as part of these Laws.

The Terms appearing on the Plan are to bear their apparent meaning, and to be deemed part of the definitions as if separately included.

Notes.

■ Indicates Post with Flag.

Length and breadth of field to be as near dimensions indicated as possible.

- - - - These broken lines indicate 10 yards distant from the half-way line and 5 yards distance from the touch-lines.

Goal dimensions—10 feet is taken from the ground to the top edge of the cross-bar and 18 feet 6 inches from inside to inside of the goal-posts.

Where practicable the intersection of the dead-ball line and touch-in goal lines should be indicated by a flag.

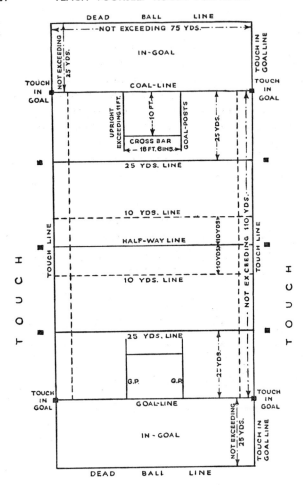

PART I.   DEFINITIONS AND GLOSSARY OF TERMS

LAW 2

The following terms have the meaning assigned to them, that is to say :

"*Beyond*" or "*Behind*" or "*In Front*" of any position indicated implies " with both feet " except when unsuited to the context.

"*Dead*" means that the ball is for the time being out of play, an event that occurs when the referee's whistle is blown, to indicate a stoppage of play, or when an attempt to convert a try is unsuccessful.

Defending Team means the team in whose half of the ground the stoppage of play occurs.

"*Fair-catch*" is obtained when a player catches the ball direct from a kick, knock-on, or throw forward by one of the opposing team if at the same time the catcher makes a mark on the ground with his heel and exclaims " Mark ".   A fair catch can be made in a player's own in-goal.   A fair catch may be obtained even though the ball on its way touches or rebounds from a goal-post or cross bar.

Field-of-Play.   The field-of-play is the space as shown on the plan, bounded by, but not including, the goal-lines and touch-lines.

Playing Enclosure.   The playing enclosure means the field-of-play and a reasonable area surrounding it.

Goal.   A goal is obtained by kicking the ball over the opponents' cross-bar from the field-of-play, by any place-kick or drop-kick except a kick-off or drop-out, without touching the ground or any player of either team.   A goal is scored if the ball has crossed the bar, even though it may have been blown back afterwards, and whether it has touched the cross-bar or either goal-post or not.   A goal is scored if the ball has crossed the bar notwithstanding a prior offence by a player of the opposing team.   A goal may be awarded if the ball is illegally touched by any player of the opposing team if the referee is of the opinion that a goal would otherwise undoubtedly have been obtained.

Grounding the Ball.   Grounding the ball is the act of a player placing his hand or hands on the ball, while it is on the ground, so that he is able to exert on it a downward pressure.

Note.—Picking up the ball from the ground is not " grounding " it.

Kick.   A kick is made by propelling the ball with the foot, or leg from the knee to the toe inclusive.

Drop-kick.   A drop-kick is made by a player in possession of the ball letting it fall from the hand or hands to the ground and kicking it at the first rebound as it rises.

Place-kick.   A place-kick is made by kicking the ball after it has been placed on the ground for that purpose.

Punt.   A punt is made by a player in possession of the ball letting it fall from the hand or hands and kicking it before it touches the ground.

Drop-out.   A drop-out is a drop-kick taken by the defending team after a touch-down or after the ball has touched or crossed the touch-in-goal or dead-ball line.

Free-kick.   A free-kick is a kick allowed for a fair catch.   It may be taken by a place-kick, drop-kick, or punt.

Kick-off.   Kick-off is a place-kick taken from the centre of the half-way line :

(*a*) at the beginning of a match,

(*b*) on the resumption of play after the half-time interval and

(*c*) after a goal has been kicked,
or a drop-kick taken at or from behind the centre of the half-way line after an unconverted try.

Penalty-kick.   A penalty-kick is a kick awarded to the non-offending team by reason of an infringement of the Laws by their opponents.   It may be taken by a place-kick, drop-kick, or punt.

Knock-on.   A knock-on occurs when the ball is propelled by the hand or arm of a player in the direction of his opponents' dead-ball line or when the ball after striking the hand or arm of a player travels in the said direction ; provided that a movement of the ball in the player's grasp which is in the nature of a steadying or readjustment of the ball within his possession without loss of control is not a knock-on.

Throw-forward.   A throw-forward occurs when the ball in the possession of a player is thrown in the direction of his opponents' dead-ball line.   A throw-in from touch is not a throw-forward.   If the ball is not passed forward but, after alighting on the ground it bounces forward, the pass is in order.

Rebound.   A rebound occurs when the ball, after striking any part of a player except his hand, arm, or leg from the knee to the toe inclusive, travels in the direction of his opponent's dead-ball line.   A rebound is not a knock-on.

Mark.   The mark is the place at which a free-kick or penalty kick is awarded.

No-side.   The end of a match.

Off-side denotes that a player is in such a position that he is out of the game, and that it is illegal for him to play the ball or interfere with an opponent.

On-side denotes that a player is in the game and not off-side.

Scrummage.   A scrummage, which can only take place in the field of play, may be either a loose scrummage or a set scrummage :

> (*a*) a loose scrummage is formed by one or more players from each team in physical contact and on their feet closing round the ball when it is on the ground between them ;
>
> (*b*) a set scrummage is formed by players from each team closing up in readiness to allow the ball to be put on the ground between them in accordance with Law 15 (B).

Tackle.   A tackle occurs when the holder of the ball in the field of play is held by one or more players of the opposing team so that while he is so held the ball comes in contact with the ground, or there is a moment when he cannot pass or play the ball in any other manner.

Touch-down.   A touch-down is obtained by the act of a defending player first grounding the ball in his own in-goal.

Try.   A try is obtained by the act of an attacking player first grounding the ball in his opponents' in-goal.

At first sight, all the above definitions and terms seem to be fairly obvious, but in match application there are one or two points which require clarification.   For instance, since the goal-posts and goal-lines are in the " in-goal area ", a try or a touch-down can be obtained by placing the ball actually on the goal-line, or in contact with the ground and a goal-post.   In the case of a fair catch, it is not necessary for a player to be standing still, or to be facing his opponents' dead-ball line, or to remain stationary after making his mark; all the same, a mark must definitely be made and *claimed simultaneously* with the catch.

PART II. PRELIMINARY

LAW 3. GROUND

All lines shown on the plan must be suitably marked out. The touch-lines are in-touch. The goal-lines are in in-goal. The touch-in-goal lines and corner-posts are in touch-in-goal. The goal-posts are to be erected in the goal-lines. Any objection by the visiting team arising in connection with the subject-matter of Laws 1 and 3 must be made before the first kick-off.

Touch judges and players, especially wing three-quarters, should remember that the touch-lines are in touch, so that the flag should be raised even though a player carrying the ball merely puts one foot on the line. It is the duty of the referee to satisfy himself before a game begins that the ground is properly marked out and that everything is in order.

LAW 4. BALL

The ball shall be oval in shape and of the following description, as far as possible :

Length in line	11 to 11¼ inches
Circumference (end on) . . .	30 to 31 inches
Circumference (in width) . . .	24 to 25½ inches
Weight	13½ to 15 ounces

For schoolboys, slightly smaller balls than the above standard size are generally used. Broadly speaking, it is a good thing for boys up to the age of fifteen to play with a " Size 4 " ball, while very young boys use still smaller ones. These are all of proportionate length, circumference, and weight to the standard ball.

LAW 5. PLAYERS' DRESS

A player may not wear dangerous projections—buckles, rings, etc. Shoulder pads are prohibited unless the referee is satisfied that a player requires protection following injury and that the protective pad is not of hard material. Any studs on his boots must be of leather, rubber, aluminium or any approved plastic, circular, securely fastened, provided the following dimensions are rigidly adhered to:

Maximum length (measured from sole) . .	$\frac{3}{4}$ inch
Minimum diameter at base	$\frac{3}{4}$ inch
Minimum diameter at top	$\frac{1}{2}$ inch

The referee has full power to decide before or during the game that any part of a player's dress, including boots and projections thereon, is dangerous and in that case must order *such* player to remove the same and not allow him to take further part in the match until after such removal.

LAW 6. APPOINTMENT OF REFEREE AND TOUCH JUDGES

In all matches a referee and two touch judges must be appointed or mutually agreed upon.

LAW 7. METHOD OF SCORING

A try	3 points
A goal from a try (in which case the try shall not count)	5 points
A goal from a free kick or penalty kick . .	3 points
A dropped goal otherwise obtained . . .	3 points

LAW 8. TIME, ETC.

In international matches two periods of forty minutes each shall be played ; in other matches the duration of play shall be

agreed upon by the respective teams, or it not agreed upon shall
be fixed by the referee.   Play shall be divided into halves.   At
half-time the teams shall change over and there shall be an
interval of not more than five minutes.   A period not exceeding
two minutes shall be allowed for any other permitted delay.   A
longer period than two minutes may be allowed only if the
additional time is required for the removal of an injured player
from the field-of-play.   Playing time lost as a result of any such
permitted delay shall be made up in that half of the game in
which such delay occurred, subject to Law 10 (8).

LAW 9

Before a match begins the captains shall toss for the right to
kick-off or the choice of ends.

In the vast majority of cases, the captain winning
the toss will choose to attack with such local advantages as sun, wind, or slope in his favour, and only
if there is nothing to be gained from these will he
elect to kick-off first.   Like so many other games, it
is generally a big psychological advantage in Rugger
to build up a half-time lead; and even with, say,
a strong wind in their faces, many a team has hung
on to such a lead with great determination.   The
sun on a winter afternoon can be a great asset; a
team can often utilise it in the first half by frequent
kicking ahead into the eyes of the opposing full-
back, and then find that after the interval the sun
has set and no longer hinders their own defenders.
A similar advantage can often be utilised by playing
in the first half with a strong wind which tends to
die down in the late afternoon.   These are all
opportunities for the shrewd captain to make the
fullest use of winning the toss.

LAW 10. FUNCTIONS OF REFEREE

(1) The referee is sole time-keeper and judge of fact, and shall keep the score.

(2) He is sole judge of Law, subject to a right of appeal to this Union.

(3) He is not entitled to contract out of the Laws of the Game by agreeing with both teams to vary or not to recognise any Law.

(4) He must not give any instructions or directions to either team prior to a match.

(5) He may, before arriving at a decision, consult the touch judges or either of them on any point of fact material to their functions, or with regard to time in the case of failure of his watch.

(6) He may not consult with anyone else, except with regard to time, and then only if the information supplied by the touch judges is insufficient.

(7) He must allow extra time for delays, subject to Law 8 and the next following clause of this law.

(8) He has power to stop a match before time has expired if, in his opinion, the full time cannot be played.

(9) In the case of his being unable to officiate during the whole period of a match, he shall have power to appoint a substitute to take his place, failing an agreement by the captains of the respective teams.

(10) He cannot alter any decision when given (except only when such a decision is given without knowledge of the fact that the Touch Judge's flag remains raised and he does not over-rule such decision of the Touch Judge).

(11) It rests with him to impose penalties for irregularities, and to give all necessary directions within the Laws. He has full powers under Law 5 both before and during the game.

(12) He must not allow anyone but the players on to the playing enclosure during a match, except with his permission.

(13) He must not allow any player to leave the playing enclosure without his permission, which should only be granted in special circumstances.

> *Note.*—Any player who, through injury or any other cause, has to retire during a match, shall not resume playing in that match until he has obtained the permission of the referee.

(14) The referee must carry a whistle. He shall blow it to indicate the beginning of a match and the resumption of play after the half-time interval. With the exception of these occasions the blowing of the whistle stops the match for the time being, and the referee shall blow it only to indicate:

(a) A try.

(b) A goal.

(c) That the ball has been touched down.

(d) That the ball has touched or crossed the touch, touch-in-goal, or dead-ball lines.

(e) A breach of Law, or irregularity of play, unless the non-offending team gains an advantage.

(f) That he is awarding a penalty.

(g) A fair-catch (even though he has blown for a knock-on or throw-forward).

(h) That the ball or player carrying it has touched him unless he considers that neither team has gained an advantage subject to Law 30.

(i) Player hurt (immediately the ball next becomes dead and subject to resumption of play, in not more than two minutes, except as provided in Law 8).

(j) Danger, when continuation of play would be dangerous.

> *Note.*—If the tackled player plays in the proper spirit and at once fairly releases the ball, very few cases of danger can arise, but by holding on for a short time danger may arise. In such cases a Referee should award a penalty.

(k) Foul play or misconduct.

(l) Half-time or no-side, as soon as the ball has become dead, except as the result of a try or the award of a fair-catch or penalty-kick, when in each case he shall allow play to proceed until the ball next becomes dead.

(m) That a stoppage is necessary for any other reason.

(15) The referee shall not whistle for an infringement during play which is followed closely by an advantage gained by the non-offending team, and for this purpose an advantage must be either territorial or else such clear possession of the ball as constitutes an obvious tactical advantage. A mere opportunity to gain an advantage is not sufficient (subject to Law 21 (Kick-off) and Law 27 (Touch)).

(16) In case of any dispute relative to a try or a kick at goal where it is possible that an appeal may be made to the Union, the referee shall allow the kick at goal, so that if the kick is successful and the Union supports the appeal, the goal points may be added.

Note.—When a kick at goal is allowed the match should be re-started as though no dispute had arisen.

It will be seen that with all the above functions to perform, a referee's job is no sinecure. Very often, the whole onus for an enjoyable game rests upon his shoulders, and, relying on the help of his two touch judges, he should do his best always to remember that. A special chapter (VIII) has been given to the control of the game, and more will be said about the referee in those pages.

LAW 11. FUNCTIONS OF TOUCH JUDGES

(1) Each touch judge must carry a flag and remain in touch, one on each side of the ground, except when a kick at goal from a try, free-kick, or penalty-kick is being taken, when both must assist the referee by standing, one at or behind each of the goal-posts of the defending team and signalling by raising his flag to indicate that the ball has gone over the cross-bar. (2) He must hold up his flag when and where the ball or the player carrying it has gone into touch, and indicate which team is entitled to bring the ball into play. (3) He must lower his flag immediately the ball has been thrown in by a player of the team entitled to do so, but if the ball is otherwise thrown in, or if the player throwing in the ball put either foot into the field of play, he must keep his flag raised, and the ball shall be thrown in again. (4) He must signal when the ball, or the player carrying it, has gone into touch-in-goal. (5) Any decision of a touch judge may be over-ruled by the referee. (6) A touch judge is under the control of the referee, who has power to deal with him as a player under Law 34 (*b*) and (*c*).

The functions of the touch judges will also be mentioned in Chapter VIII; and that completes

B

what the laws call the " preliminaries ". We now come to :

PART III. THE PLAY IN DETAIL

LAW 12. NUMBER OF PLAYERS

A match shall be played by not more than fifteen players in each team. Any objection by either team in connection with this Law may be made at any time, but it shall not affect any score previously obtained.

LAW 13. MODE OF PLAY

A match is started by a kick-off, after which any player who is on-side may, at any time, catch, kick, pick up or drop the ball, run with the ball, fall on the ball, or tackle an opponent holding the ball, except as provided for in Laws 15 and 16. The ball may be passed or knocked from one player to another, provided it is not passed, knocked, or thrown forward by hand or arm.

This last paragraph is so simple in print yet so difficult to the beginner in practice. As most learners are small boys, it is one of the hardest lessons for them to learn that progress in Rugger has to be made by passing backwards; and this apparent paradox constitutes a problem which all coaches of the young have to solve for themselves. Once a boy has realised that he must make a reasonable amount of forward progress before passing backwards, a big step has been taken; and the all-too-familiar sight of a young three-quarter line actually losing ground because their forwards have successfully obtained possession of the ball in a scrum will rapidly disappear. This simply stated law means in effect that Rugger is *the* game in which backing-up counts most, and there are few finer sporting sights than to see a well-trained Rugger team making progress down the field by means of a whole series of short individual dashes interspersed with quick, short, backward passes to supporting colleagues following up on either flank of the player in possession.

LAW 14.   KNOCK-ON OR THROW-FORWARD OR REBOUND

A knock-on occurs when the ball is propelled by the hand or arm of a player in the direction of his opponents' dead-ball line or when the ball after striking the hand or arm of a player travels in the said direction ; provided that a movement of the ball in the player's grasp which is in the nature of a steadying or readjustment of the ball within his possession without loss of control is not a knock-on.

A throw-forward occurs when the ball in the possession of a player is thrown in the direction of his opponents' dead-ball line.   A throw-in from touch is not a throw-forward.   If the ball is not passed forward but, after alighting on the ground, it bounces forward, the pass is in order.

A rebound occurs when the ball after striking any part of a player except his hand, arm or leg from the knee to the toe inclusive, travels in the direction of his opponent's dead-ball line.   A rebound is not a knock-on.

In the case of a throw-forward or a knock-on the ball shall be brought back to the place of infringement and a scrummage formed there, unless

(*a*) A fair-catch has been allowed, or
(*b*) The opposing team gain an advantage, or
(*c*) The ball is knocked-on by a player who is in the act of charging down the kick of an opponent, or
(*d*) The ball is unintentionally knocked-on by a player who is in the act of catching it direct from a kick and is recovered by that player before it has touched the ground or another player, or

(*e*) The throw-forward or knock-on is, in the opinion of the referee, intentional, in which case he shall award a penalty-kick at the place of infringement.

The fair-catch from a knock-on is an opportunity which is probably not appreciated sufficiently by the ordinary club player. Against a really tough defence, when every attempt at a break-through has been frustrated by good solid tackling, many opportunities for making a mark in the opponents' twenty-five are liable to occur. Admittedly it requires extraordinarily quick thinking to make a mark when the ball is unexpectedly propelled into one's arms, and the natural reaction nine times out of ten is to accept the sudden gift and streak away in a counter-attack. Yet against a stubborn defence in the final few minutes of an even game, the fair-catch can be a real match-winner, and it might well be practised more in school and club Rugger, where excitable forwards are liable to kick too far ahead in an effort to clear the ball from the vicinity of their own goal-line.

LAW 15. SCRUMMAGE

A scrummage, which can only take place in the field of play, may be either a loose scrummage or a set scrummage:

(*a*) A loose scrummage is formed by one or more players from each team in physical contact and on their feet closing round the ball when it is on the ground between them.

(*b*) A set scrummage is formed by players from each team closing up in readiness to allow the ball to be put on the ground between them in accordance with Law 15 (B).

(A) This part of Law 15 applies in the case of every scrummage, whether it is a " loose " scrummage or a " set " scrummage.

It is illegal for any player, except as provided by Law 26 (*b*) :

(*a*) To return the ball into a scrummage by hand or foot, or

(*b*) While the ball is in a scrummage, to handle it or pick it up by hand or legs, or

(*c*) Intentionally to cause the scrummage to collapse, or

(*d*) Intentionally to fall or kneel in the scrummage, or

(*e*) While lying on the ground to interfere in any way with the ball in a scrummage, and not do his best to roll away from the ball.

(B) This part of Law 15 applies only in the case of a " set " scrummage, i.e., one ordered or taken in accordance with the Laws.

Note.—In this part of Law 15, the terms, " first ", " second ", " third ", etc., when applied to a player, or a foot, in either front row of a scrummage refer to the position of such player or foot (the feet not being crossed or otherwise moved from their normal position), counting from the side on which the ball is being, or has been, put in ; and the term " the middle line " means an imaginary line on the ground directly beneath the line formed by the junction of the shoulders of the players forming the respective front rows.

Forming a Scrummage

(1) It is illegal for either team wilfully to delay the formation of a scrummage.

(2) Every scrummage shall be formed as nearly as practicable to the place of infringement and so that the middle line is as nearly as practicable parallel to the goal lines until the ball has been put in.

(3) Each front row of a scrummage shall be formed by three players, and it is illegal for any player at any time to add himself to a front row so formed. Subject to this any number of players may form a scrummage. The head of a player in a front row shall not be next to the head of a player of the same team.

(4) (*a*) The players of each front row shall bind firmly and continuously while the ball is being put in and while it is in the scrummage. Neither arm of the second player, nor the inner

arms of the first and third players may be free. The second player may bind either over or under the arms of the first and third players, but in either case he must bind firmly around the bodies of these players at or below the level of the armpits. The first and third players must bind the second player in like manner. (*b*) All other players in a scrummage must bind with at least one arm and hand around the body of another player of the same team.

(5) It is illegal for a front row to form down some distance from its opponents and rush against them. Such dangerous play also infringes Law 34 (*a*) (3).

Putting the Ball into the Scrummage

(6) The team not responsible for the stoppage of play shall put in the ball. A stoppage may be caused without any infringement by either team. Only when in doubt as to the responsibility, the Referee shall order the ball to be put in by the team in whose half of the ground the scrummage is to be formed.

(7) The ball shall be put in without delay as soon as the two front rows have closed together.

(8) The player putting in the ball shall

(*a*) Stand one yard from the scrummage and midway between the two front rows.

(*b*) Hold the ball with *both* hands midway between the two front rows at a level midway between his knees and his ankle and from that position in a single movement put the ball in *straight* along the middle line at *moderate* speed so that it first touches the ground immediately beyond the nearer first player.

(9) It is illegal for any player by placing or advancing or raising a foot or feet, or in any other way, to prevent the ball from being put into the scrummage, or first touching the ground in the required manner.

(10) The ball shall be put into the scrummage again if it enters and comes out at either end of the tunnel or if, on its way out, it passes between the first and second feet of either front row.

Heeling from the Scrummage

(11) It is illegal for any foot of either front row to be raised or advanced until

(*a*) In the case of either first foot, the ball has passed that foot, or (*b*) In the case of either second foot and the nearer third foot, the ball has been touched by or passed either fourth foot, or

(*c*) In the case of the further third foot and the feet beyond the ball has left the hands of the player putting it in.

(12) It is illegal for any player of either front row while heeling or attempting to heel the ball or at any time during the scrummage to

(*a*) Advance both his feet beyond the middle line, or
(*b*) Raise both his feet off the ground at the same time, or
(*c*) Swing both feet together in any direction, or
(*d*) Lower or twist his body so as to get nearer to the ball,

or in a manner liable to cause the scrummage to collapse.

Penalty.—For any infringement of Law 15 a penalty kick shall be awarded. If a player repeatedly infringes, the Referee MUST deal with him under Law 35 (*c*).

The above Law is a rather long and tedious one, and it is one which has been repeatedly amended in the interests of the game. Even now, in its present form, it is not entirely satisfactory. Many critics, for example, still maintain that it is a physical impossibility for the hooker to raise one foot and hook the ball back in the fraction of a second available after the ball has left the scrum-half's hands. They claim that a slow-motion camera would show up these deficiencies in the Law, and certainly the problem of getting the ball into a set scrummage to the satisfaction of both players and spectators is not yet finally solved. Referees—and all forwards, for that matter—are advised to study the following diagram and note when the ball is and is not fairly in the scrummage. The same principle applies to the 3–4–1 formation.

Referees are also warned to see that when a scrummage is ordered, one team does not gain ground at the expense of the other before the ball is available to re-start the game; if they do so, the scrummage should be brought back to the original place. Another point to remember in school Rugger is that the referee has no authority to permit delay because a player has not succeeded in getting his head down in the scrummage.

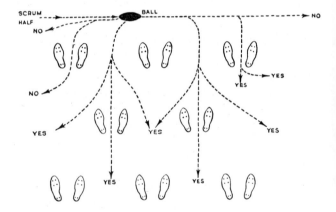

LAW 16. TACKLE

A tackle occurs when the holder of the ball in the field-of-play is held by one or more players of the opposing team so that while he is so held the ball comes in contact with the ground, or there is a moment when he cannot pass or play the ball in any other manner.

(a) When a player is tackled but not brought to the ground, he must *immediately* release the ball.

(b) The tackled player, if lying on the ground, must *immedi-*

ately release the ball, roll away from it, and get up before playing it.

(*c*) It is illegal for any player (i) to prevent a tackled player from releasing the ball, or getting up after he has released it, or

(ii) to attempt to pick up the ball before a tackled player lying on the ground has released it, or

(iii) while lying on the ground after a tackle to interfere with the ball in any way.

The foregoing provisions are subject to Law 26 (*d*).

Penalty.—Penalty-kick awarded at the place of infringement. If a player carrying the ball is thrown or knocked over, but not tackled, he may, nevertheless, pass the ball or get up and continue his run, even though the ball has touched the ground. See italicised words in Law 10 (14) (*j*).

It is left entirely to the referee to decide whether or not a player is properly tackled. If he is of the opinion that a tackle *has* occurred, he must insist on the ball being released immediately. Any struggling for the ball should be stopped, either by the awarding of a penalty-kick, if the referee is able to judge which team is responsible, or by a scrummage if he is unable to do so. The first part of this Law—" after a tackle the ball must be brought into play with the foot "—is a difficult thing in practice for the beginner. So often the ball goes loose after a tackle, and a keen but inexperienced young forward dashes up, picks it up, and scores what he considers an opportunist try. He must, however, learn to curb this natural impulsiveness and remember that before picking up the ball he must play it—the merest touch is sufficient—with his foot.

LAW 17. LYING ON THE BALL

A player lying on the ground with the ball in his possession, or in such a way that he prevents an opponent from gaining possession of it, must immediately play the ball, or get up, or roll away from the ball.

Penalty.—Penalty-kick awarded at the place of infringement.

This Law is really designed for the protection of the players themselves. If a plucky young outside falls on the ball in order to stop a forward rush by his opponents, it is obviously in his own interest to get up or roll away as quickly as possible ; otherwise he is likely to be injured as his opponents try to play the ball. The art of falling on the ball is, incidentally, one which becomes perfectly clear as soon as it has been demonstrated by an expert ; although it looks a risky procedure, there is really little danger if it is done properly. Teachers and coaches will do well to bear this in mind.

LAW 18. OFF-SIDE

(1) When the ball is in play, except in a scrummage or in a line-out, a player is off-side if the ball has been kicked or touched or is being carried by one of his own team behind him.

It is illegal for a player who is off-side under this part of Law 18, and who has not become on-side under Law 19, to :

(*a*) Play the ball (except when receiving an unintentional throw forward), or

(*b*) Obstruct an opponent in any way, or

(*c*) Approach or wilfully remain within ten yards of an opponent *waiting* to play the ball.

It is illegal for any player to shout " all-on-side ", or words to that effect, when any member of his team is off-side.

Penalty.—Penalty-kick awarded at the place of infringement, or, at the option of the non-offending team, a scrummage at the place where the ball was last played by the offending team. If such latter place is in in-goal, the scrummage shall be formed five yards from the goal-line on a line through the place parallel to the touch-lines. When a penalty kick is awarded for illegally shouting from in-touch, the kick shall be awarded ten yards from the touch-line, on a line through the place parallel to the goal-lines.

When an off-side player is unable to avoid being touched by the ball, or by a player carrying it, he shall be deemed to be "accidentally off-side" and a scrummage shall be formed at the place where he was so touched.

(2) While a scrummage is forming or is taking place, a player is off-side if

(a) He enters a scrummage from his opponents' side, or

(b) Being in front of the ball and not in the scrummage he fails to retire behind the ball without delay, or

(c) Not being in the scrummage, he advances either foot in front of the ball in the scrummage.

A player is not in a scrummage unless he is binding with either arm a player of his own team in the scrummage.

Penalty.—Penalty-kick awarded at the place of infringement.

(3) While a line-out is taking place in accordance with Law 27 a player is off-side if

(a) Before the ball has touched a player or the ground he wilfully remains or advances with either foot in front of a line at right angles to the touch-line through the place where the ball went into touch, unless he advances solely in the act of jumping for the ball, or

(b) After the ball has touched a player or the ground he, not being in possession of the ball, advances with either foot in front of the ball, unless he is lawfully tackling or attempting to tackle an opponent who is participating in the line-out. Such tackle or attempt to tackle must, however, start from his own side of the ball.

It is not intended that a player before throwing in the ball should be obliged to wait until players of his own team have returned to or behind the line-out, and a player is not to be deemed as wilfully remaining under Law 18 (3) (a) provided he so returns without delay.

Penalty.—Penalty-kick awarded at the place of infringement or ten yards from the touch-line on a line at right angles to the touch-line through the place where the ball went into touch, whichever is the farther distance from the touch-line.

LAW 19. ON-SIDE

(1) A player who is off-side under Law 18 (1), *including* a player to whom Law 18 (1) (*c*) applies, becomes on-side :

(*a*) When one of his own team has run in front of him carrying the ball, or

(*b*) When one of his own team has run in front of him after having kicked the ball when behind him. Such kicker must be in the field-of-play or in in-goal to put the off-side player on-side, though he is not debarred from previously following up in touch or in touch-in-goal, or

(*c*) When he has retired behind the player of his own team who last played the ball.

(2) A player who is off-side under Law 18 (1) *other than* a player to whom Law 18 (1) (*c*) applies, becomes on-side

(*d*) When an opponent carrying the ball has run five yards, or

(*e*) When the ball has been kicked or passed by an opponent, or

(*f*) When an opponent has *intentionally* touched the ball, provided such opponent does not catch or gather it.

Referees are asked to note that a penalty-kick should not be given against a player who over-runs the ball when it is in the scrummage if he immediately tries to get back behind the ball. Similarly, no penalty should be incurred unless the offside player attempts to play the ball or interfere with an opponent. This word " interfere " is reasonably elastic, and an off-side player may approach an opponent waiting for the ball up to a distance of 10 yards from him ; if, however, he advances to within, say, 6 yards, he automatically incurs a penalty.   In that case the referee should whistle at once, because delay might prove dangerous to the player waiting to receive the ball.

LAW 20.   CHARGING AND OBSTRUCTION

It is illegal for any player

(*a*) Who is running for the ball to charge an opponent also running for the ball, except shoulder to shoulder, or

(*b*) Who is not running for the ball to charge or obstruct an opponent not holding the ball, or

(*c*) Who is overtaking an opponent also running for the ball to push him from behind, or

(*d*) To hold an opponent who is not carrying the ball. Pulling any part of the clothing of an opponent should be dealt with as holding under this Law and under Law 34 (*a*) (2).   Players should, however, not be penalised for " holding " if they drag away a player lying on the ground in close proximity to the ball but not in a scrummage.

(*e*) With the ball in his possession after it has come out from a scrummage or a line-out to attempt to force his way through players of his own team in front of him, or

(*f*) Who is off-side wilfully to run or stand in front of another player of his own team who is in possession of the ball, thereby preventing an opponent from reaching the latter player, or

(*g*) Being an outside player in a scrummage, to move outwards when the ball has been obtained by his team and is emerging from the back of the scrummage, thereby preventing an opponent from advancing round the scrummage, or

(*h*) Who is not himself running for the ball wilfully to charge or obstruct an opponent who has just kicked the ball.

Penalty.—(1) For any infringement of (*b*) and (*d*) of this Law the penalty provisions of Law 34 (*a*) and (*b*) apply.

(2) For other infringements : penalty-kick awarded at the place of infringement : provided that in the case of infringement of (*h*) the opposing team shall have the option of taking the kick at the place of infringement or at the place where the ball alights.

If the ball alights in touch the mark shall be at a place

ten yards from the touch-line on a line parallel to the goal-lines through the place where it crossed the touch-line.

If the ball alights within ten yards of the touch-line the mark shall be at a place ten yards from the touch-line on a line parallel to the goal-lines through the place where it alighted.

If the ball alights in in-goal, touch-in-goal, or over or on the dead-ball line, the mark shall be at a place five yards from the goal-line on a line parallel to the touch-line through the place where it crossed the goal-line or ten yards from the touch-line, whichever is the greater.

One of the commonest forms of obstruction occurs during a scrummage when a wing forward moves outwards to protect his scrum-half and enable him to get the ball away unhampered. Even if he still maintains contact with the rest of the scrum, the wing forward must still be penalised, and referees are instructed to regard such an action as " obstruction ". It should be noted that if two players on different sides are chasing the ball after a kick ahead, a shoulder-to-shoulder charge is permissible, but no pushing or holding is allowed in such a case. There is an unfortunate tendency nowadays, only partly due to excessive keenness, for players to push or hold opponents in the line-out before the ball arrives ; this law now authorises the referee to award a penalty-kick at once for such tactics.

LAW 21.   KICK-OFF

Kick-off is a place-kick taken from the centre of the half-way line or a drop-kick taken at or from behind the centre of the half-way line.

(a) A place-kick must be taken from the centre of the half-way line or after an unconverted try a drop-kick must be taken at or from behind the centre of the half-way line; otherwise the ball shall be kicked off again.

(*b*) The ball must reach the 10-yards line unless first played by an opponent, otherwise it shall be kicked-off again or a scrummage formed at the centre, at the opponents' option. If it reaches the 10-yards line and is then blown back, play shall continue.

(*c*) The kicker's team must all be behind the ball; otherwise a scrummage shall be formed at the centre.

(*d*) The opposing team must not stand within 10 yards of the half-way line; otherwise the ball shall be kicked off again.

(*e*) The opposing team must not charge until the ball has been kicked; otherwise the ball shall be kicked off again.

(*f*) If the ball pitches in touch, touch-in-goal, or over or on the dead-ball line, the opposing team may accept the kick, have the ball kicked off again, or have a scrummage formed at the centre.

Law 10 (15) as to advantage does not apply in the event of any of the foregoing not being complied with.

The main point to note here is that the ball must reach the 10-yards line *unless first played by an opponent.* In other words, it is permissible for an opposing player to dash forward and collect a short kick, even though the ball may have travelled only a few yards over the half-way line. Beginners should also note that play must continue once the ball has crossed the 10-yards line, even though a strong wind should blow the ball back again. The advantage of a kick-off can be nullified by a forward who is keen to back up crossing the half-way line just before the kick has been made; for this reason, it is a good tip for the kicker's forwards to line up a few yards *behind* him, instead of running up level with him. With a strong following wind, it is often a big territorial advantage to kick a long ball well down towards the opposing goal-line. In such circumstances the kicker must remember that the ball must pitch inside certain limits; a long kick which sails over the touch-line or dead-ball line usually results in the opposing captain selecting a scrum back at the centre.

LAW 22. DROP-OUT

A drop-out is a drop-kick taken by the defending team after a touch-down or after the ball has touched or crossed the touch-in-goal or dead-ball line.

(a) A drop-kick must be taken from anywhere on or behind the 25-yards line; otherwise the ball shall be dropped out again.

(b) The ball must reach the 25-yards line; otherwise the opposing team may have it dropped out again or have a scrummage formed at the centre of the 25-yards line. If it reaches the 25-yards line and is then blown back, play shall continue.

(c) All the kicker's team must be behind the ball when kicked; otherwise a scrummage shall be formed at the centre of the 25-yards line.

(d) The opposing team must not charge over the 25-yards line; otherwise the ball shall be dropped-out again.

(e) If the ball pitches in touch, the opposing team may accept the kick, or have the ball dropped-out again, or have a scrummage formed at the centre of the 25-yards line.

Law 10 (15) as to advantage should be applied in the event of any of the foregoing not being complied with.

This law is quite easy to understand and quite simple in practice. The only common mistake is the old one of players who *will* persist in getting in front of the kicker. It seems extraordinary that this bad habit applies just as much to first-class matches as it does to school games; in every class of Rugger there is to be found the pseudo-keen player who is too lazy—mentally or physically—to apply to himself the simple rule that he must keep behind the ball at a drop-out or a kick-off. A few words on this subject from the captain before a game or at half-time might save a lot of unnecessary stoppages.

LAW 23. FREE-KICK

Note.—A free-kick is a kick allowed for a fair-catch. It may be taken by a place-kick, drop-kick or punt.

(*a*) A free-kick must be taken at or behind the mark, on a line through the mark parallel to the touch-lines ; the kick must be taken by the player making the fair-catch, and the ball must reach a line through the mark parallel to the goal-lines, unless first played by an opponent.

(*b*) In the case of a place-kick, the ball must not be handled by the kicker after it has been placed on the ground.

(*c*) In every case the kicker's team, other than the placer for a place-kick, must be behind the ball when the kick is taken, and may follow up. The opposing team may come up to, but not beyond, a line through the mark parallel to the goal-lines, and may charge subject to the following conditions :

(i) In the case of a place-kick, as soon as the ball has been placed on the ground.

(ii) In the case of a drop-kick or punt, as soon as the kicker begins his run or offers to kick.

Note.—When a free-kick has been awarded if players of the opposing team, having charged fairly, prevent the kick from being taken, the kick is void and play should be recommenced only by a scrummage at the mark, the opposing team having the right to put in the ball. If the mark is in in-goal it shall be deemed to be on the goal-line and the ball must cross that line unless first played by an opponent : otherwise the kick must be taken again.

Penalty.

(i) For infringements by the kicker's team—a scrummage at the mark.

(ii) For infringements by the opposing team—charge disallowed ; if the kick has been taken, the kicker shall be allowed the option of another kick under the original conditions without the charge.

Law 10 (15) as to advantage should be applied in the event of any of the foregoing not being complied with.

Note.—If a player who has made a fair-catch is injured in so doing and is unable to take the kick within two minutes, the kick is void, and a scrummage shall be formed at the mark. If the mark is in in-goal, the scrummage shall be awarded 5 yards from the goal-line on a line through the mark parallel to the touch-lines. When a player is placing the ball neither he nor the kicker shall wilfully do anything which may lead the opposing team to charge before the ball has been placed on the ground ; in the event of either doing so, the charge shall not be disallowed.

According to the definition, a free-kick is a kick allowed for a fair-catch, and it may be taken by a place-kick, drop-kick, or punt. In actual practice, a section of this Law—(*c*) (i)—makes place-kicking a somewhat risky procedure, while punts are generally reserved for touch-finding. Consequently, most free-kicks well in the opponents' half of the field take the form of drop-kicks aimed at goal ; and the actual kicker should remember that as soon as he begins his run or " offers " to kick, his opponents may charge from the line through the mark.

LAW 24. PENALTY-KICK

Note.—A penalty-kick is a kick awarded to the non-offending team by reason of an infringement of the Laws by their opponents. It may be taken by a place-kick, drop-kick or punt.

A scrummage may be taken at the mark by the non-offending team in lieu of a penalty-kick. When a penalty-kick is taken the following provisions shall apply :

(*a*) A penalty-kick must be taken at or behind the mark, on a line through the mark parallel to the touch-lines. The kick may be taken by any player of the team, and for a place-kick the kicker may place the ball. The kick must be taken without undue delay.

(*b*) The ball may be kicked in any direction, but may not be played again by the kicker until it has been played by another player. If, however, the kicker has indicated to the referee that he intends to attempt a kick at goal, it is illegal for him to kick the ball in any other way.

(*c*) In every case the kicker's team, other than the placer for a place-kick, must be behind the ball until it has been kicked.

(*d*) All players of the opposing team must retire without delay to or behind a line parallel to the goal-lines and ten yards from the mark, or to their own goal-line if nearer to the mark, and there remain motionless with their hands by their sides until the ball has been kicked.

(*e*) It is illegal for any player of the opposing team to prevent the kick from being taken or to interfere with the kicker in any way while he is taking the kick.

Penalty.

(1) For an infringement by the kicker's team—a scrummage at the place where the ball was kicked, subject to Law 33 (*b*).

(2) For an infringement by the opposing team a penalty-kick ten yards in front of the mark or on the goal-line, whichever is the nearer, on a line through the mark parallel to the touch-lines.

Law 10 (15) as to advantage should be applied in the event of any of the foregoing not being complied with.

The recent change in (*b*) above, the ball now not necessarily having to be kicked towards the opponents, has brought into play the " short penalty ", when the ball is tapped back with the foot to another player, who may then be able to start an attacking movement.

LAW 25. PLACE-KICK AT GOAL AFTER A TRY

After a try has been scored, the scoring team shall have the right to take a place-kick at goal on a line parallel to the touch-lines through the place where the try was obtained but need not take the kick. The kicker may place the ball.

(*a*) All the kicker's team must be behind the ball when kicked.

(*b*) The opposing team must be behind the goal-line until the kicker begins his run or offers to kick, when they may charge or jump with a view to touching the ball.

(*c*) The kick must be taken without undue delay.

Penalty.

(i) For an infringement by the kicker's team—the kick shall be disallowed.

(ii) For an infringement by the opposing team—the charge shall be disallowed; or, if the kick has been unsuccessfully taken, the kicker shall have the option of another kick under the original conditions without the charge.

Neither the kicker nor any player placing the ball for him shall wilfully do anything which may lead the opposing team to charge prematurely; in the event of either doing so the charge shall not be disallowed.

There are one or two points in connection with this law which affect the technique of a place-kicker. First of all, the ball must be in contact with the ground; if the kick is taken while the ball is still held in the placer's hands above the ground, the referee must declare the kick void, and no second kick is allowed. Secondly, although the kicker is permitted to make adjustments in the direction and angle of the ball while it is still in the placer's hands, once it has been placed on the ground, the kicker is not allowed to handle it; if he does so, the referee is instructed to disallow the kick. Thirdly, shouting by the defending team during a kick at goal must be treated as " misconduct ", and if no goal is scored in such an event, another kick should be allowed without the charge. Finally, it should be remembered that the kick at goal after a try is optional. Thus, if a side have just scored a vital try far out near the corner flag on a muddy day a few minutes before the end of an even game, they can save precious time by not bothering about the kick at goal; in that case, the game must be re-started by a drop-kick from the centre.

LAW 26. TRY

Note.—A try is obtained by the act of an attacking player first grounding the ball in his opponent's in-goal.

A touch-down is obtained by the act of a defending player first grounding the ball in his own in-goal.

A try is scored in the following cases :

(*a*) If a player passes, knocks, or kicks the ball into his own in-goal and an opponent first grounds it.

(*b*) If a team in a scrummage pushes the other team over the latter's goal-line and first grounds the ball in in-goal. If the defending team grounds it, a touch-down shall be awarded.

(*c*) If a player grounds the ball in his opponent's in-goal and picks it up again, a try shall be awarded where it was first grounded.

(*d*) If the momentum of a player when held in posses-sion of the ball carries him into his opponents' in-goal and he first there grounds the ball, even though it has touched the ground in the field-of-play.

The referee shall award a try if, in his opinion, one would undoubtedly have been obtained but for the unfair play or unlawful interference of the defending team. Such try shall be awarded between the posts. (See also penalty under Law 34 (*a*) and (*b*).)

A try may be scored by a player who is in touch or in touch-in-goal, provided he is not carrying the ball. When the referee cannot decide which team first grounded the ball in in-goal, a scrummage shall be formed 5 yards from the goal-line opposite the place where the ball was grounded, and the attacking team shall put in the ball.

Referees and beginners should specially note section (*b*) of the above law, since this is the only occasion when a player is allowed to touch the ball with his hands in a scrum. It is, moreover, a very satisfying method of scoring a try, to push the opposing eight firmly over their own goal-line while nursing the ball carefully in the second or third row of the scrum. Note also that in whichever part of the field or in-goal area the ball is when a " penalty try " is awarded, that try is regarded as having been scored between the posts, so that the penalty will in all probability be five points.

LAW 27.   TOUCH

(*a*) The ball is in touch :

(i) When, not being in the possession of a player, it touches or crosses a touch-line, or

(ii) When, being in the possession of a player, it or the player carrying it touches a touch-line or the ground beyond it.

If the ball crosses a touch-line and is then blown back it is in touch at the place where it first crossed the line.

A player may be in touch and yet play the ball with his foot if the ball is not in touch.

(*b*) The ball must be brought into play by an opponent of the player whom it last touched in the field-of-play, unless such player carrying the ball is physically forced into touch by an opponent, in which case it shall be brought into play by the player so forced or by one of his team.

In the event of the Touch Judge being unable to decide which team should bring the ball into play, the referee, if being himself in doubt, shall order the ball to be brought into play by the team in whose half of the ground it has gone into touch.

(*c*) The ball must be brought into play at the place where it went into touch by throwing it into the field-of-play so as to touch a player or the ground at least 5 yards from and at right angles to the touch-line.

If thrown in otherwise the opposing team shall have the right, at its option, to throw in the ball or to take a scrummage. If on the second occasion, the ball is not thrown in correctly a scrummage shall be formed. Any scrummage so taken or ordered shall be formed 10 yards from the place where it went into touch on a line parallel to the goal-lines.

Law 10 (15) as to advantage does not apply in the event of the foregoing not being complied with.

A player throwing the ball in from touch must not put either foot into the field-of-play, otherwise the ball shall be thrown in again.

(*d*) Until the ball has been thrown in and has touched a player or the ground as provided under (*c*), it is illegal for any player participating in the line-out wilfully to

    (i) Be off-side, contrary to Law 18 (3) (*a*), or
    (ii) Push, charge, shoulder or bind with or in any way hold another player of either team, or
    (iii) Use any other player as a prop to enable him to jump for the ball.

(*e*) After the ball has touched a player or the ground it is illegal for any player participating in the line-out to

    (i) Be off-side, contrary to Law 18 (3) (*b*), or
    (ii) Hold, push, shoulder or obstruct an opponent not in possession of the ball, or
    (iii) Charge an opponent otherwise than in an attempt to tackle him or to secure possession of the ball.

If the ball in a line-out becomes unplayable, otherwise than as the result of an infringement for which a penalty is prescribed, the referee shall order a scrummage.

Penalty.—In the event of an infringement of (*d*) or (*e*) or of Law 35 a penalty-kick shall be awarded at the place of infringement or ten yards from the touch-line on a line through that place at right angles to the touch-line, whichever is the farther distance from the touch-line.

It is possible that a player may deliberately throw the ball in " not straight " from touch, especially if his side prefer scrums to line-outs; in such cases the referee should award a penalty-kick. Note also that if the ball fails to reach the 5-yards broken line, the procedure is the same as when it is thrown " not straight ", and a scrum 10 yards in from the touch-line must be given. It is possible, too, for a player to run up from behind the line-out and take the ball in his stride if there is a gap, but should he run into another player of *either* team while doing this, a penalty-kick must be awarded against him for charging. Finally, wing three-quarters must remember to keep both feet in touch when they are throwing in.

LAW 28. WILFUL THROWING INTO TOUCH, ETC.

If a player wilfully knocks or throws the ball from the field-of-play into touch, touch-in-goal, or over his own dead-ball line, the opposing team shall be awarded a penalty-kick at the place where such knock or throw occurred.

LAW 29. TOUCH-IN-GOAL

The ball is in touch-in-goal :

(*a*) When, not being in possession of a player, it touches a corner-post, or touches or crosses a touch-in-goal line.

(*b*) When the ball in a player's possession, or a player carrying it, touches a corner-post or touches a touch-in-goal line or the ground beyond it.

The flag shall not be regarded as part of the corner-post.

LAW 30. BALL, ETC., TOUCHING REFEREE

If the ball or a player carrying it touches the referee in the field-of-play, a scrummage shall be ordered at that place, unless the referee considers that neither team has gained an advantage, in which case he shall allow play to proceed.

When a scrummage has been ordered the team of the player who is carrying the ball, or last played the ball, shall put in the ball.

If the ball in a player's possession, or a player carrying it, touches the referee in that player's in-goal, a touch-down shall be awarded ; and if the ball, while in play in in-goal at either end, but not held by a player, touches the referee, a touch judge, or a spectator, a touch-down shall be awarded, provided that a touch-down would otherwise have been obtained, or the ball would have gone dead ; and if the issue is in doubt when the ball touches a spectator, a touch-down shall be awarded the visiting team, provided they are the defending team.

If a player crosses his opponents' goal-line with the ball in his possession and, before grounding it, touches the referee, a try shall be awarded at that place.

If the ball, while in play in in-goal at either end but not held by a player, touches the referee, a touch judge, or a spectator, a try shall be awarded at that place, provided an attacking player would otherwise have scored it ; and if the issue is in doubt when the ball touches a spectator, a try shall be awarded at that place to the visiting team, provided they are the attacking team.

The implication of this Law is to throw the onus for the orderly behaviour of spectators on to the shoulders of the home side. In any doubtful cases, if the ball strikes a spectator who has encroached into the in-goal area, the referee should award a touch-down to the visiting team if they are defending, or a try if they are attacking.

LAW 31.   BALL HELD IN IN-GOAL

If a player in possession of the ball in in-goal is so held that he cannot ground the ball a scrummage shall be formed 5 yards from the line opposite the place where he was held and the attacking team shall put in the ball.

LAW 32.   TAKING BALL OVER GOAL-LINE

If a defending player heels, kicks, passes, knocks or carries the ball over his own goal-line and it there becomes dead except in the case where a try is obtained or as provided for in Law 26 (*b*) or in Law 28 a scrummage shall be formed 5 yards from the goal-line opposite the place from which it was kicked, passed, knocked or carried back and the attacking team shall put in the ball.

A drop-out shall be awarded if as the result of a kick, pass or knock by an attacking player the ball on its way touches a defender who does not wilfully attempt to stop (otherwise than in an attempt to nullify a dropped goal), catch or kick it and crosses his goal-line and

(*a*) Is there made dead by a defender, or

(*b*) Crosses the dead-ball line or touch-in-goal line.

LAW 33.   INFRINGEMENTS IN IN-GOAL, ETC.

The referee must disallow a try and award a touch-down if in his opinion a try would undoubtedly not have been gained but for unfair play or unlawful interference on the part of the attacking team.

Subject to Law 26 of Law 34 for infringements in in-goal the penalty shall be :

(*a*) For an offence by the attacking team—a touch-down, or

(*b*) For an offence by the defending team—a scrummage 5 yards from the goal-line opposite the place of infringement.

LAW 34.   FOUL PLAY, MISCONDUCT

The following are prohibited :

(*a*) Foul play, including—

(1) Wilful hacking, tripping, or striking.

(2) Wilfully holding a player not in possession of the ball.

(3) Illegal tackling (including early and late tackling and dangerous tackling).

(4) Illegal pushing, charging or obstructing.

(5) Wilfully causing a scrummage to collapse.

(*b*) Misconduct while the ball is in play.

Penalty.—The referee shall either order the offending player off the playing enclosure or else caution him and, in addition, shall award a penalty kick at the place of infringement (subject to Law 20 (*h*)).   For a second offence the referee MUST order the player off.   If the foul play or misconduct prevents a try which, in the opinion of the referee, would *probably* have been scored he shall award a penalty try between the posts.

(*c*) Misconduct, including unlawful interference, while the ball is out of play.

Penalty.—The referee shall either order the offending player off the playing enclosure or else caution him and shall, in addition, award a penalty-kick, which may be taken at any place where the ball would next have been brought into play, if the infringement had not occurred. If such a place is on the touch-line the kick shall be taken at a point 10 yards from such a place on a line parallel to the goal-line. For a second offence the referee MUST order the player off. If ordered off, under the provisions of Laws 34 or 35, the player shall take no further part in the match in progress and the referee MUST, without delay, send a report, naming the player and describing the incident:

(*a*) To the Constituent Body to which the player's club is affiliated or allotted to;

(*b*) To the Rugby Football Union if more than one Constituent Body is concerned.

(*c*) To the R.F.U. if the club of the player is not affiliated or allotted to a Constituent Body;

(*d*) To the International Board in International matches (in each case forwarding a copy of his report to his own Referee Society);

(*e*) To the R.F.U. if he himself does not belong to a Referee Society.

LAW 35. REPEATED INFRINGEMENT OF THE LAWS

(*a*) Where a player infringes for a second time any of the provisions of Law 34—the referee MUST order the player off the playing enclosure.

(*b*) When a player repeatedly infringes any of the provisions of Law 20 the referee MUST order him off the playing enclosure.

(*c*) When a player repeatedly infringes any of the Laws other than Laws 20 and 34 the referee MUST caution him and *must* in the event of any further repetition of the infringement in respect of which the caution was given, send a report naming the player and the circumstances to the Constituent Body having jurisdiction over the Club to which the player belongs.

(See last paragraph of Law 34.)

LAW 36. WASTE OF TIME

Waste of time, caused intentionally by any player, or by a team, including the wilful infringement of any Law or Laws for which the penalty is only a scrummage, is illegal.

Penalty.—Penalty-kick awarded at the place of infringement. Repeated infringements *must* be dealt with under Law 35.

LAW 37. IRREGULARITIES NOT PROVIDED FOR

When a law is broken or any irregularity of play not otherwise provided for occurs, and an advantage is gained therefrom by the opposing team, the referee shall not blow his whistle, but shall allow the match to continue ; but if no advantage is gained by such team and if no other procedure is provided, the ball shall be taken back to the place where the breach of the Law or irregularity occurred and a scrummage formed there.

The above thirty-seven laws cover everything which can reasonably be allowed for in a game of Rugby football. If the reader is really keen and determined to teach himself this game, he will now, having studied the laws theoretically, go and watch them being put into practice in a match. If he follows the referee carefully, he will soon be able to associate the somewhat heavy legal phrases of the laws with the actual playing of the game itself. At the same time, of course, if he is young enough to do so, he will be adding weekly to his knowledge of the game by playing it as regularly as possible. Yet even in the case of experienced Rugger stalwarts, it would undoubtedly lead to a general improvement in the game if they made it a rule at the beginning of each new season to sit down and read solemnly through the laws. A player would in truth be a real expert on the game if his hour's reading did not result in some increase in his knowledge of Rugger.

APPEALS
on Referees' Decisions on Points of Law
(Law 10 (16))

Clubs are requested to notice that when they desire to make an appeal on points which have occurred in a particular match, before forwarding the Appeal to the Secretary of the Rugby Football Union the statement should be submitted to the Referee for his views to be expressed on it.

CHAPTER IV

BASIC PRINCIPLES

A. KICKING

THERE are three main types of kick in Rugger—the punt, the drop-kick, and the place-kick. While the drop- and place-kicks are more specialised for certain members of the fifteen, every player should be able to punt accurately and quickly. Far too often a player finds the ball in his possession in his own twenty-five and tries to punt to touch, but miskicks into the hands of an opponent. Let us see how this can be rectified.

The Punt. The method of punting a Rugger ball is very similar to that used by a soccer goal-keeper. The oval ball must be held with the long axis pointing downwards, and the aim is to bring the curve of the instep in contact with the curve of the middle of the ball. Let us analyse the stages of a punt with the right foot. First grip the ball correctly with the hands rather above the middle of the sides than below. Take a few paces forward, reaching a steady run, see that your body is firmly balanced on the left foot, with the weight rather forward and the ball held out in front, and then bring the right foot forward with a swing, keeping the knee bent. At the same time release the ball without throwing it

up, straighten the leg so that the foot is snapped
forward and upward to meet the ball, keep the toe
pointed downwards, and allow the leg to follow
well through in the direction of the kick. Keep
both eyes on the ball the whole time and practise
punting with both right and left feet.

Punting Practice. Beginners should always aim
for quickness and accuracy rather than for length.
A group of three players, A, B, and C, position

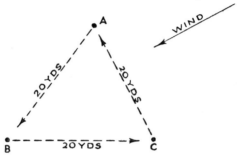

themselves about 20 yards apart. If there is any
appreciable wind, the best kicker—in this case B—
should kick against it. The object is to kick the
ball round the triangle without it hitting the ground.
As you catch the ball, readjust your grip to the
correct one, turn to face the next player as rapidly
as possible, and then make a calm, unhurried kick.
After a few rounds in one direction, A → B → C,
reverse it. Then try a round of left-foot kicks.
Finally, when you can complete the circuit without
grounding the ball, increase the distances to 30
yards. A good practice for two players, especially

if they are full-backs, is to kick to each other across a touch-line, as in the accompanying diagram. Two posts are placed 20 yards from the touch-line.

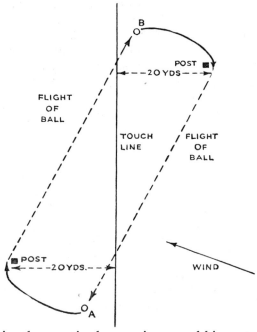

A begins the practice by running round his post and punting left-footed to B, who catches the ball, swerves round his post, and finds a similar " touch " near A. Try to select your line so that the wind does not favour either of the kickers. For right-foot punting, move each post to the opposite side of the touch-line.

The Short Punt Ahead. This is a valuable skill for three-quarters, but it must be perfected in order to be more useful than harmful. The object is for a player A, when running towards an opponent B, to kick over his head in such a way that by swerving round B, A has a good chance of gathering the ball again before another opponent, generally the full-back, can field it. The kick is only a short one, usually not more than about 15 yards, but it has to be made without the run being checked. The ball is merely dropped on to the kicking foot and is kicked quite near the ground. You can practise this alone by trying to kick the ball up in front of you and then catch it as it descends. Alternatively, you can start on one side of the goal-posts, kick over the cross-bar, and chase the ball on the other side. If you cannot catch the ball before it pitches, a lucky bounce should be gathered in your hands gratefully, but in the case of an unlucky bounce try to carry on with your feet in a dribble. Sometimes it pays to make a long punt ahead, especially if the ball can be kicked accurately to a strategic place undefended by the opposition, but an outside who regularly kicks straight into the hands of the full-back is a menace to his side!

The Cross-kick. This is another type of punt, usually delivered at right angles to the direction in which the player is running, and is not unlike a centre from the wing at soccer. A typical cross-kick occurs when a wing three-quarter runs up the field close to and parallel with the touch-line; when

c

in the vicinity of his opponents' 25-yard line, he punts the ball by swinging his leg across the body so that the ball travels high in the air and pitches about 20 yards out from the goal-posts. Two other players should follow down the centre of the field in anticipation, taking care to keep on-side. It requires considerable practice if this kick is to be made accurately when the wing three-quarter is really running fast.

The Drop-kick. Before the 1948–49 season a dropped goal counted four points, but it is now the same value as a try. Nevertheless, a stand-off half and the two centres should be good drop-kickers; and in any case the game has to be re-started after a touch-down or an unconverted try by means of a drop-kick. The movements are practically identical to those of a punt, except that the ball is released sooner so that it is just in the act of bouncing off the ground by the time the foot is swinging forward. It is important to hold the ball straight in front of the kicking foot and to hold it so that the long axis is nearly vertical; in that way the ball will bounce slightly backwards on to the moving foot. Once again it is necessary to keep the head down and to follow well through.

Timing a Kick. In every game when a ball is to be hit by a moving bat, club, stick, racket, or foot, the moving object should just be accelerating as it hits the ball. Because the ball is slightly compressed by the impact, it is always in contact with that moving object for a short but definite period of time. During that brief period there must be an acceleration and not a slowing up, in order to give the maximum force or " punch " to the ball. This is generally referred to as " good timing ". When kicking, therefore, the foot should be travelling at its fastest immediately after impact with the ball.

Place-kicking

There is a feeling among older Rugby players that place-kicking is a lost art, and there is certainly a shortage of reliable place-kickers nowadays. Yet it is difficult to see why this is so, for in these days of many penalty kicks, games can be won or lost by good or bad kicking; and it is something which you really can " teach yourself ". There are three main types of place-kick—the penalty-kick at goal, the attempted conversion of a try, and the kick-off.

The Penalty-kick. Exactly how to take a penalty-kick is a matter for you to work out on your own; each kicker is sure to develop his own technique. There are, however, certain basic principles common to all. First, if you should be given a penalty-kick 10 yards from your opponents' line and wide out near the touch-line, do not forget that you can take the ball back in a straight line to widen the angle. Having selected your spot, turn your back on the goal-posts, and dig your heel into the turf to make a hole. If the ball is greasy or muddy, wipe it on the grass—or your shirt!—before placing it in the hole. It is here that there are most individual differences; some players always stand the ball upright, and although this may be best for short kicks, for longer ones it is usually better to slope the ball away towards the goal. If you are kicking against a strong wind, you must lay the ball down almost flat and aim to kick it just over the bar; if you kick it high, the wind will only blow it about.

Having " placed " the ball, walk back for your run and wipe the mud off your kicking boot. First-class kickers usually pause for a long moment at this stage, concentrating on the job in hand as they stare at the spot on the ball they mean to kick. Then take three or four steps, so spaced that, if you are kicking with the right foot, the instep of your left foot comes down level with the ball, and, swinging your leg straight, kick the ball in the middle with your toes. Follow straight through without checking your swing; and, above all, remember that golden rule of all ball games, " keep your eye on the ball ". This means that you must resist the temptation to lift your head and eyes a split second before your foot connects with the ball. Even after you have kicked the ball, it is a good tip to go on looking at the spot from which it was kicked. You must, of course, allow for any cross-wind; only with experience will you learn exactly how much to aim off.

Converting a Try. This is similar to a penalty-kick except that as soon as the kicker begins his run or offers to kick, your opponents are allowed to rush you from behind their goal-line. As before, first select your spot and make a hole; this must be in a straight

line back from the place where the try was scored,
the exact spot being indicated by the referee dig-
ging his heel in the turf. The distance you go
back from the goal-line will naturally depend on
how far you can kick; if you are a strong kicker,
you might go back to the twenty-five line in order

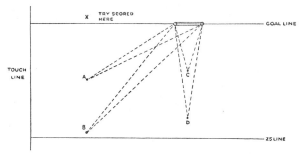

A = Weaker kicker, short distance, narrow angle.
B = Strong kicker, longer distance, wider angle.
C = Easy conversion from 10 yards, wide angle, but fear of
    opponents charging the kick.
D = More difficult conversion from 20 yards, narrower angle,
    but no fear of opponents charging the kick.

to widen the angle as much as possible. If the kick
is straight in front of goal, it is preferable to choose
your spot as close to the posts as possible, without
getting so close that your opponents can charge
down the kick; the closer you are, the wider your
" angle of error " and the less time the wind has
to affect your kick.

Bearing the above advantages and disadvantages
in mind, we will assume that you have now chosen

your spot and made your hole as before. In this "cup" you carefully adjust the ball at the angle and direction you want it to be; then you kick as for a penalty.

The Kick-off. As a rule, enough care is not taken over the kick-off from the centre spot. Too often the kicker boots the ball rather aimlessly among the opposing forwards, and one of them has ample time to catch it and either start a movement or make a long touch. If your opponents are not well positioned,

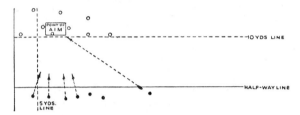

then by all means try to obtain a bounce into touch inside their twenty-five line, but normally it is better to aim at a spot just beyond the 10-yards line and about 5 to 10 yards in from touch. Try to kick the ball as *high* as you can, for this gives your forwards more time to reach the opponent who is catching it.

In order to obtain as much height as possible, make a shallow hole in the turf with your heel, place the ball almost upright, and with a run of only two or three steps, kick the ball with your toes as near the ground as you can. In that way, you get your foot under the ball and "spoon" it up to a fair height. Meanwhile, your forwards are following up rapidly, in the hope that one of them at least will arrive at the same time as the ball; if they can do this at the very beginning of a match it has a definite psychological effect.

B. CATCHING THE BALL

Catching or fielding is a vital part of a full-back's play, but sooner or later every member of a fifteen will have to field a ball coming through the air towards him, just as every member of a cricket eleven is expected to hold his catches. It is poor play by any side to allow a ball kicked by their opponents to bounce, unless, of course, it is kicked over all their heads and away from the full-back. Once a Rugger ball has been allowed to hit the ground, it may bounce anywhere, so every effort should be made by the nearest player to get under it. If two players are near together, one of them should avoid a muddle by calling " Yours " or " Mine " as soon as possible.

Many of the essential points in catching are the same as in cricket, but there is one vital difference. If you drop your catch at Rugger but do not knock the ball forward, you have a chance of recovery; you can pick up the ball and carry on. If, however, you " knock-on "—that is, allow the ball to bounce forward off your arms—a scrum will follow at that place, and you will have lost your side many valuable yards. Try to position yourself right under the falling ball, so that you do not have to catch it with outstretched hands, and aim to hug it between your arms and your chest. If possible, stop running before you make your catch and take a firm stance. Keep your eyes on the ball, and do not look at any opponents rushing towards you. Hold your hands with a gap of about 6 inches between them and slightly above the level of your elbows; this makes a wide cradle into which the ball should safely fall. Many inexperienced catchers fail because they leave too big a gap between their elbows. If a strong wind is blowing or if the ball is spinning, its flight will be irregular, so you must be ready to move your feet so as to shift your " cradle " a few feet according to the final movement of the ball.

After you have made your catch safely, the following moves are possible :

(1) Return the ball to touch by means of a punt.

(2) Open up the game by running with the ball so that your colleagues can form up alongside you and a passing movement can be initiated.

(3) If you are about to be tackled, pass the ball immediately back to a colleague.

(4) Make a " mark ".

(5) If it is within your range, take a drop-kick at goal.

Whenever you are practising catching, each of the above five possibilities should be imagined. For (1) and (2) it is essential to move quickly to one side or the other, in order to dodge any opponent rushing towards you. Making a quick side-step after the catch, you will soon find how easy it is to beat an opponent who is following up, but after your side-step make sure of your kick if you are a fullback.

The Mark or Fair Catch. When a player about to make a catch is certain that he will be unable to dodge the several opponents who may be rushing towards him, he should " make a mark ". At the moment of catching the ball, he must place his heel firmly in the ground and call " Mark ". The referee, if satisfied, will blow his whistle, and the game stops. The opponents are then allowed to come up as far as the mark, and the player who fielded the ball must move back about 10 yards, so that, allowing for his opponents to rush forward immediately he moves, he can still punt over their heads. Compared, therefore, with a normal return punt, the player who makes the mark loses at least 5 yards of ground; but when you are in a tight corner, it allows your side to get back in support and so is a valuable form of defence.

C. PICKING UP THE BALL

The game of Rugger was meant to be played with the ball being handled, and the shape of the ball makes that far more possible than if it were round. A rolling Rugger ball is always liable to bounce up to such a position that it can be gathered by the hands, and to be able to do this while on the run is a valuable asset to any player. It is therefore worth while to teach yourself this art by practice. The main essential is one of agility, to be able to run while bending down so that your hands are only about 18 inches off the ground. A simple practice is to run normally, then bend forwards and put your two arms down, not straight in front of you, but to right or left of your feet. Run about ten paces in that position and then straighten up again.

Next, place a ball on the ground about 6 or 8 yards in front of you. Run forward, bend over with your arms down on the right side, and pick up the ball; you will be facing half-right, and your arms can easily sweep across your body. If you are naturally right-handed, you will find this the easier way; if left-handed, you should gather on the left side. After that, roll the ball in front of you, and when it is about 4 yards ahead run after it and pick it up. If you have a partner, get him to roll the ball either towards you or across your line of running.

Finally, practise dribbling and picking up *a dry ball*. As mentioned in the section on dribbling, outsides as well as forwards should practise dribbling, but they should try to do it in such a way that they have a reasonable chance of gathering the ball in their hands. There is a definite knack in this, to persuade the ball to roll over and over with the long axis in a vertical plane, like this:

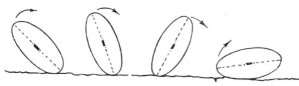

This can be done by dribbling more with your shin-bones than with your feet. As the ball continues rolling in this way, it gathers speed, and will probably bounce up to such a height that the hands can gather it fairly easily. This dribbling and gathering can be carried out in games whenever a pass goes astray and the feet have to be used, or whenever a kick ahead is made. No one-man movement is prettier to watch than a player who makes a short punt ahead over his opponents, carries on with a dribble because he does not get a lucky bounce, but finally gathers the ball again to go over for a try.

All players should know what their capabilities are for picking up a ball, so that they realise their own limitations. Many a dribble is spoilt by a player trying to pick up the ball and giving a knock-on. A golden rule is : never try to pick up a *wet* ball. When opponents are dribbling, there is often an opportunity for defending outsides to pick up the ball, especially when it is kicked too far ahead. On the other hand, if you fail in your attempt to scoop up the ball, the dribble may become dangerous, and it would have been better to have fallen on the ball and so made certain that the dribble was stopped. So be sure you know your limitations, and do not attempt to risk more than that.

D. TACKLING

Much the best advice for learning to tackle is to start young and with others of your own size and strength. Once you are fully grown, cold-blooded tackling practice is rather a grim business! All the same, there are many who have been playing the game for a few years and have yet to learn to tackle. The following is a suggested procedure. Assuming that you wear gym shoes, choose a soft or grassy piece of ground, and have a partner of your own size and weight:

Stage I—Standing Jumps. A is going to tackle B. B should stand still, with both feet apart, while A should stand at a distance of his own height from B and in the direction shown in the accompanying figure. A then takes a standing dive (such as

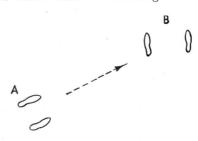

would produce a " pancake " dive into water) with the object of getting his shoulder against some part of B's leg between the hip and the knee. At the moment when the shoulder meets B's leg, both A's legs should be off the ground, and this impact should knock B off his balance. To make certain that B will fall over and not merely run away, A's arms should be wrapped round B's legs so that they grasp him as they both fall. The important point to remember is that it is not merely the arms but the *shoulder's impact* that constitutes a tackle. It is then B's turn to tackle A, after which A should have another go, this time using the other shoulder.

Stage II—The Running Take-off. This really represents the advance from a standing dive to a running dive. A is to tackle B from behind. This is the easiest position, because no timing is required so long as A can catch up B. B moves forward at walking or slow running pace, and A overtakes him and at a suitable distance makes his dive. Then interchange as before and practise using both shoulders. The wearing of gym shoes should prevent any unpleasant kicks as the tackler dives forward.

The Cross Tackle

This tackle is made almost at right angles to the direction in which the opponent is moving, and it is the most commonly used by outsides. It is essential to use the correct shoulder so that your head does not get squashed between the ground and a player on top of you. Therefore when moving to the left, use the left shoulder, and vice versa. More accurate timing of your jump is now necessary, since if you are too late in starting you will just have no legs against which to break your fall! Some players make a slight variation by almost allowing their opponents to go past them and then they tackle from behind; while this makes the actual tackle easier, the timing has to be even more precise. If you intend to carry out these tackling exercises on one another, it is best to get thoroughly warmed up first by other forms of practice.

Tackling Practice for Many

For boys under fourteen, a good tackling game is a form of " Tom Tiddler's Ground ". According to the number of players available, an area between the goal-line and a 25-yard line is marked off by posts or flags. Two of the best tacklers stand in the middle, while the others have to run from goal-line to twenty-five line without being brought down. Anyone who is thus tackled has to stay in the middle and tackle the others until only one—the winner— is left. In the case of young boys, the tackler has not far to fall even if he dives and misses; but as soon as the same boys reach manhood, leading-up games do not appeal so much to them, and if the practice is going to represent the pace of an actual game, the " tacklee " tends to suffer more bumps than the " tackler ".

For this reason, various devices of lifeless " tacklees " have been invented, usually taking the form of stuffed sacks. The difficulty is to make the sack sufficiently heavy without being too large in circumference, and yet filled with soft material. So choose a tall, narrow sack and fill it with old clothes or sacking rather than with straw. Whatever device is used, the main object is the same—to instil confidence. Once you have the same confidence in diving at the legs of an opponent as you have in diving into a swimming-bath, the defensive part of the game of Rugger becomes as attractive as the attacking part.

There is sometimes a tendency for forwards to regard tackling as a job entirely for the outsides, but every member of a fifteen must play his part in stopping any opponent within his reach from carrying the ball. Because of the congestion which occurs at a line-out, a forward often has to tackle an opponent who is quite close to him; there is no chance of a running dive. In that case the shoulder must still be put firmly against your opponent's leg below his waist. At the same time your arms should close rapidly round him, so that you prevent him from passing the ball.

Avoiding a Tackle

This technique is inevitably linked up with the previous section, in which the victim who offers himself to be tackled is presumed to walk or run straight until he is brought down. He should be determined to try to free himself if possible and not be like some victims, who collapse before they have been really tackled. In a proper game, the tackler will come up against various devices which, unless his tackling is resolute, will probably foil him.   The chief of these devices is:

The Hand-off

A player holding the ball may thrust away any opponent with the open palm of his hand, but not, of course, with his clenched fist.   A right-wing three-quarter should grasp the ball in his right arm so that he will have the left free for the hand-off. This left arm is first bent so that the hand is almost up to the face, and the hand is then swung down as the arm is straightened.   Another way of describing the thrust is to consider the arm action when a vault is made over a gate.   The left hand is placed on the gate, and a downward thrust, which straightens the arm, gives an uplift to the whole body, thus helping it over the gate.   Note that there is just one thrust with the arm for one opponent; it must, therefore, be made at the correct moment.

The player with the ball, in order to judge this moment accurately, must watch his opponent like a cat watching a mouse;   immediately he sees him start his dive, he should thrust down his open hand. If the tackle is about waist high, the left hand will be able to meet the tackler's head or face and thrust it away.   In actual practice, a strong hand-off will give a push-off just like that when vaulting over the gate.   The only way to tackle a player who can give a strong, well-timed hand-off is to keep below the reach of his hand, so the best height at which to aim your tackle is just above the knees.

Other Ways to Avoid a Tackle

The swerve and the side-step are the recognised ways by which a runner with the ball can carry himself just far enough away from an opponent to be out of reach of his tackle. The details for the foot movements for these evasive runs will be described later, but it should be realised that, for a player to make use of a swerve, he should first be able to move *towards* his opponent so that he can then swerve to either side. From the tackler's point of view, it is best for him to watch not the eyes or hands of his opponent but his feet. Such bad faults as running across or running back in order to avoid tackles should always be avoided; the same applies to the risky action of " jumping over " an opponent as he dives to tackle.

E. FALLING ON THE BALL

If the opposing forwards are coming down the field with the ball at their feet, there are only two ways to stop them. The first—and the best if they kick it far enough forward—is to race across their advancing front and whip the ball off their toes. When they are keeping it close, however, and especially when the ball is wet, the only way to halt their advance is to fall on the ball.

Now it requires a good deal of courage to throw yourself at a ball dribbled by hurrying feet; it is less often realised that it also takes skill. Correct timing is the crux of the matter; choose a moment when the dribbling forward has least control of the ball, and dive. You should try to throw yourself over the ball and present your curved back to the feet of the advancing forwards. As you hit the ground you may whip the ball into your stomach with your hands, but you must then *instantly* release it. You must never lie on top of the ball, otherwise you will concede a penalty. The attacking forwards will usually trip over you, and a good place for your hands at this rather uncomfortable stage is clasped behind your head, with your forearms over your ears and your elbows protecting your face.

Once you have thrown yourself down in this manner, it is important to roll clear as soon as possible. Modern referees will award a penalty-kick if you hang on to the ball for an instant, or if you lie on top of it, or if you obviously make no real effort to roll clear. Therefore everyone should realise that falling on the ball can only check but not halt a forward rush, and forwards must gather round in support as quickly as they possibly can. Consequently, it is important to fall with your body between the ball and the feet of the opposing forwards, for this makes it much easier for your side to form a loose scrum and heel the ball back. Your opponents must either first pull you away from the ball or else hook it over your prostrate body.

There is one other occasion when the safest thing to do is to fall on the ball. That is when the ball has been kicked over your head and you are rushing back towards your own line to retrieve it, with an opponent on your heels. If you fall on the ball just as you reach it, your pursuer will trip over you and you may then jump to your feet with the ball and kick for touch. The player most concerned with this technique is the full-back.

F. EQUIPMENT

Fortunately, Rugby football is not an expensive game to play, and even in these days you can equip yourself well for a few pounds. It is worth buying a pair of good boots, for cheap ones may barely survive a hard season's wear and tear. Buy proper Rugby boots, of course; they are black and more supple than the brown soccer boots. Some firms make different boots for outsides and forwards; the outsides' boots are specially adapted for speed in running, while the forwards' are stiffer, to give more holding power for shoving in the scrum. Rugby studs are usually a little longer than soccer ones and taper more towards the end. It is a good thing to have six studs in each sole; this gives a good grip when swerving, and it cannot be too strongly emphasised that outsides especially should imme- diately replace any loose or lost stud. It pays to take real care of your boots; remove all the mud after each game, then allow them to dry and clean them with ordinary blacking. See that no nails are sticking through, either into your foot or out through a stud, which might accidentally injure another player.

If you wish, you can insert a shinguard or some cardboard under your stockings to give you some protection from minor kicks; if you do, see that you have some efficient way of keeping your stockings up! Shorts should be as strong as possible, and it is an advantage if they have pockets because you can often use a moment of waiting to warm cold hands. Shorts should be kept up by a tape; if you rely on elastic, you are liable to be " debagged " during a tackle or loose scrum! No metal buckles are allowed, for the obvious reason that they may cause an accident.

The jersey will normally be supplied by your club. It needs to be big enough for comfort; in almost every dressing-room you can see at least one player who requires two team-mates to peel off his jersey! The collar should be as strong as possible; the lace-up neck-line worn by some soccer players would receive short shrift in the scrums. The second-row and lock forwards should wear scrum caps; these have pads over the ears to ensure that they will not be rubbed until they are sore. The hooker should always wear shin-pads, since he is likely to receive frequent bruises down the front of his leg. And everybody, but particularly the outsides, should possess a pair of mittens— gloves with the fingers cut out—for use when the ball is slimy.

CHAPTER V

USEFUL PRACTICES

RUGGER is often referred to as " a man's game ". By that phrase, its keenest enthusiasts claim that it is a hard, healthy sport in which there is no place for the weakling or the coward; and up to a point they are right. Yet the very word " weakling " is capable of different interpretations in sport. As an extreme example, a big powerful forward who thinks nothing of his own physical fitness or makes no attempt to master the elementary arts of dribbling, passing, and catching the ball can often be a weakling in the sense that he is a definite liability to his team in the last half-hour of a hard-fought game. No Rugger player has ever reached international standards without putting in hours and hours of practice, and if you, the reader of this book, really do wish to teach yourself the game, you must be prepared to start in a humble way and learn the fundamentals gradually.

Admittedly many club players are busy people who regard each Saturday match as an opportunity for a pleasant game, but a player's improvement will be very slow if he relies entirely on match play to develop his skill. Yet if you join a club which runs a number of teams, the best way in which you can win promotion for yourself to the senior fifteens is to show a keenness in practice which is certain to bring satisfactory results in matches. Unfortunately for the keen young player, it is not very easy for him to take a Rugger ball and go out on to a field once or twice a week in order to carry out practice by himself; even if it were, it would be a somewhat boring procedure. But in the following pages a number of " purposeful " games have been enumerated, and each of these practices is designed to improve the player's standard in one particular phase of Rugger in as pleasant and jolly a manner as possible, always assuming he can persuade a number of colleagues to join him. For the reader's convenience, these games have been collected into a number of groups, under the headings of quickness off the mark, swerving, kicking, dribbling, passing, and, finally, combined skills.

A. Quickness off the Mark

This " skill " is, of course, an extremely useful one for any Rugger player, but it is particularly valuable to those who play outside the scrum. The object is to develop maximum speed for those vital first 5 yards, and anything which a player can do to encourage this asset will pay ample dividends on the field of play.

One simple exercise is to have an even number of players trotting round a circle of 8 to 12 yards radius marked out on the ground. Each alternate player, A, C, E, etc., has a Rugger ball, and when the coach or captain gives a sharp blast on the whistle, A swerves 3 yards away from the circle, B dashes up at full speed on the line inside A, and A, with a short, snappy pass, slips the ball into B's hands. At the same moment, C is passing to D, E to F, and so on, according to the number of couples. All players now slow down to a gentle trot, and when the whistle goes a second time, B, D, and F swerve away from the circle, A, B,

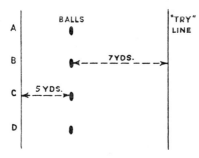

and C dash inside them, the balls are transferred, and the players slow down again. Half a dozen repeats of this quickening exercise are quite sufficient at any one time.

A good competitive game to encourage quickness off the mark is illustrated by the above diagram.

Players A, B, C, and D line up as shown about 12 yards from a " try " line marked out on the ground. In front of each player, about 5 yards away, is a Rugger ball lying on the ground. When the coach blows his whistle, they all dash forward, play the ball gently with either foot—as if it had gone loose after a tackle—pick it up, and hurtle over the line for an imaginary try. The coach can easily judge the winner by standing on the end of the " try " line. A simple knock-out competition on these lines will often provide useful information to a captain, quite apart from the intrinsic value to the players themselves.

For larger numbers of players, an adaptation of " City Gates " is recommended. This is a game

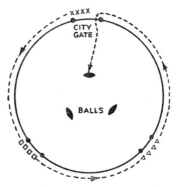

which is often played during physical-training periods in schools, and its object is to combine team-work with quickness off the mark and passing. A team of, say, four players lines up in its city gate, which is merely a couple of flags or cricket stumps 3 yards apart on the edge of a circle of 7 to 10 yards radius. A Rugger ball is placed on the ground 6 yards inside the circle from each city gate. The players turn towards a flank, and at a signal from the coach begin trotting round the circle, each team in the same direction. When all have gone about half-way round, the whistle goes again, every player dashes forward as fast as he can to complete the remainder of the circle, the leader of each team swerves through his city gate, picks up his ball, carries out a quick bout of passing with each of the remaining members, and finally, when all have participated, he darts forward in an attempt to score a try outside the circle before the leaders of the other teams can do so. As soon as the game has been played a couple of times, and the players have developed some snappy backwards-and-forwards passing, the enthusiasm rapidly increases. Each player can take it in turn to be the leader.

In addition to the above-mentioned games, every physical-training book will give a comprehensive list of similar quickening exercises, most of which can be played as simple relays in a large room or gymnasium. Lots of these can be adapted to serve the purpose of the keen Rugger player, whose aim should be to get into his stride with the least possible delay. At the same time he should realise that it is an advantage to be able to stop dead, turn round, and rush off in the opposite direction; such a movement may be a serious strain on the leg and thigh muscles, so the speed at which practice is carried out should be gradually increased after a gentle start.

B. Swerving

For the purposes of this chapter, " swerving " will be regarded as any method of running round or past an opponent; consequently, it will include feinting, dodging, side-stepping, " jinking ", and similar skills. And since in Rugger the object in swerving is to get both man and ball past an opponent, the reader who is keen enough to practise any of the following exercises should always have a ball tucked under one arm; otherwise he might automatically try to use that arm for balancing purposes.

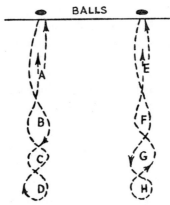

The principles of swerving can best be learned by a series of simple relay races. Teams line up behind each other, as in the accompanying diagram, roughly 6 yards apart and 6 yards between each player. When the whistle goes, A and E dash forward, pick up the ball which is lying on the ground just beyond the " try " line in front of each team, race back, swerving in and out of each member of their own team, and so back to score an imaginary try. The moment A and E are back again in their original places, B and F go through the same manœuvre, followed by C and G, and so on to the end of the team. The winning team is the one which scores the final try first.

The old game of "follow-my-leader" can be adapted to teach Rugger swerving, if played as a team game. The leader of each team, with a Rugger ball under one arm, swerves about on any portion of the field at a fairly good speed, while

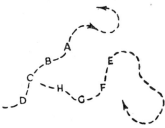

his colleagues form a "crocodile" behind him. When the coach blows his whistle, the second players, B and F, in the crocodiles dart almost alongside their leaders, A and E, receive a short pass, and immediately assume the leadership, while A and E tack on to the end of the column behind D and H. Five seconds later, the whistle goes again; C and G spurt forward to receive the ball and become leaders, while B and F fall to the rear; and so on. The important point is that the temporary leader must always keep on swerving and darting about, even to the extent of dodging through another team. In fact, a dozen players divided into three teams can get a good deal of fun in a gymnasium, provided that the coach blows his whistle frequently and does not allow the game to drag out.

Probably the standard method of practising swerving is to run in and out of a series of corner-flags or posts, which are usually placed in a straight line about 6 or 8 yards apart. A better method is to make it into a competitive swerving relay by

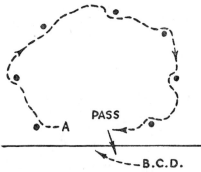

arranging the obstacles in a kind of horseshoe, and making each player run round the course with a Rugger ball, which he passes on to his next colleague at the end of his run. While A is making his run, it is a good idea to have B, C, and D waiting behind a line, so that after he has swerved round the last obstacle, A gives a backward pass to B, who by this time is running alongside him. In a similar way B transfers the ball to C, and C to D, so that with two or three identical " horseshoes ", the whole practice can become a competitive team-race.

A similar swerving relay which incorporates a short punt ahead can be practised by setting up the obstacles as in the accompanying diagram. As soon as the whistle goes, the first player, A, races forward from the line, and after passing obstacle No. 1 he makes a short punt ahead, catches the ball in his stride, and proceeds to swerve round and

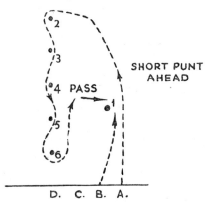

through obstacles 2, 3, 4, 5, and 6. At this point B joins him by running alongside, and at obstacle No. 1, A passes the ball to B, who in turn punts ahead, catches it, swerves through the obstacles, passes to C, and so on. As in all these relays, with two or three teams competing, the practices can become most exciting as the last three runners come swerving back to dive over the line for the final winning " try ".

The last stages in teaching yourself to swerve should be carried out with a friend in order to correlate swerving and passing. A simple exercise is for each pair to trot gently down the field, inter-passing after first selling the dummy.

The above movement is, of course, an exercise, or perhaps " drill " would be a better word, and it should be carried out at first quite slowly. Then, as the two players fall into the drill, it can be done faster and faster, until the slight swerves are made at top speed—dummy, pass, receive . . . dummy, pass, receive . . . and so on. Once this manœuvre has been mastered, it automatically leads on to the scissors movement. In order to teach this as a drill, remember that the man with the ball always runs across the front of his partner.

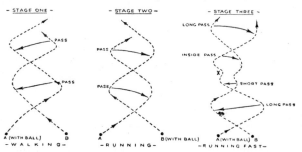

Scissors passing and swerving can best be taught in three stages. The first stage is to carry it out at a walking pace, slowly at first and then briskly, always being careful to pass *backwards* to your partner. If A starts on the left with the ball, all passing will be from right to left, as in the first diagram. The second stage is to carry out the manœuvre while running, all the passes being still given from one side, that is, from left to right in the second plan. Once the principle of the scissors movement has been grasped, the third stage is to vary the drill as much as possible. For instance, the first pass might be a long one by A, the second merely a gentle 1-yard lob by B, as A crosses immediately behind him. Then at the point X, player A might swerve *outwards* instead of inwards, a cue for B to run straight ahead to receive a normal pass. B might then run across field before sending a long pass to A. In other words, two keen players, with an occasional call of " Outside You " or " On your Right ", can develop, by a simple series of practices, a real understanding and produce some quite bewildering manœuvres. Of course, this is all done in practice, and it is quite a different matter to apply these exercises in an actual match. Yet there is no doubt that a real feeling of confidence can result from such a systematic course of training, and all games players realise only too well that confidence is a tremendous asset during match play. These scissors movements apply particularly to those who play in the three-quarter line.

C. Kicking

There are three kinds of kick in Rugger which it is possible for a keen player to practise, and they are the ordinary place-kick at a stationary ball, the drop-kick, and the punt. For many players, unfortunately, the only opportunities for improvement are those which present themselves during an actual match or at the informal " punt-about " before a game begins. Yet for those who are able to spend a short time each week in practice, the main object should be to develop accuracy in kicking. Place-kicks, drop-kicks, and punts all need to be carried out accurately if they are to serve their purposes during a match, and in that connection it is worth remembering that in modern Rugger almost as many points are scored with the foot as with the hand.

Quite a fair proportion of club players, especially the valuable heavy but rather clumsy forward type, literally do not know how to drop-kick. Yet ten minutes' practice with a toy balloon or soccer bladder will enable such a player to teach himself the fundamental principles of the art. Stand quite firmly on one foot and swing the other leg rhythmically forwards and backwards, pointing the toes but keeping the whole leg straight from the thigh downwards. Just as the instep is about to skim over the ground, at the lowest part of the forward swing, say to yourself " drop " . . . " drop " . . . " drop ". Then repeat this movement while holding a *round* ball, balloon, or bladder in both hands in front of the body. Drop this object just as the instep is completing its descent, and as the ball leaves the ground, the foot will swing through its

RUGBY FOOTBALL
IN
ACTION

Top : A Harlequin player tries to fall on the ball as P. W. Kininmonth
(Richmond and Scotland) leads a forward dribble.
Bottom : T. Allan (Wallabies) shows good form in a dive over the London
Counties' line to score a try.

Top : Lt. J. Matthews (Army and Wales) goes for the Navy line with great resolution.
Bottom : Three Harlequin forwards well to the fore in a line-out against Richmond.

Top : A scrum-half throws out a long pass.
Bottom : R. Uren, England's full-back, shows the moment of impact as he attempts to convert a try against Scotland.

A later stage of another conversion—a good high kick.

An England stand-off half about to start a three-quarter movement against Wales.

Top : An early stage in the formation of a loose scrum.
Bottom : A. F. Dorward (Cambridge and Scotland) gets the ball out to Glyn Davies (Cambridge and Wales) from a scrum on the half-way line.

arc of the circle, establish contact, and propel the ball on its way. Keep the head down throughout the operation, and very soon you will be able to judge the exact moment to release the ball from the hand. If the release is too soon, the ball will be kicked high into the air, probably with the lower part of the shin. Do not throw the ball forward; it is literally a " drop ".

Once the drop-kick has been mastered with a round ball, it is no great step to manage it with a Rugger ball. Hold it at an angle of about twenty degrees from the vertical, so that as the oval-shaped ball falls and rebounds, it will fit neatly into the instep. As soon as you are reasonably proficient, go out on to the field with a friend, stand about 10 yards away from each other and practise drop-kicking gently but accurately. A drop-kicks to B, who catches the ball and drop-kicks back to A, and so on. Aim for each other's faces, and as you become more and more proficient, lengthen the distance between you. The next stage is to practise drop-kicking over the actual goal, one of you standing on the twenty-five line, and the other on the dead-ball line. Finally, do it on the run as you move laterally across the front of the goal; and you can drop-kick like that with either foot, your practice will have been well worth while.

The next type of kick is the punt. Any footballer can punt a Rugger ball if he is standing still and not aiming at a specific target, but to punt on the run and hit a definite objective is quite a

D

different problem. An ordinary " punt-about " is quite good fun, but it does not improve one's accuracy; consequently, the determined player must be prepared to put in a certain amount of rather grim practice if he wishes to become really proficient at punting. Go out on to the field with a colleague and, from a stationary position, punt accurately to each other over short distances; later on, you can increase this length, but at the very outset it is important to realise that accuracy is at all times preferable to length, especially when it is a question of finding touch. In match play, the short punt over an opponent's head is a very valuable kick, particularly if it is controlled in such a way that the kicker can run round his opponent and catch the descending ball in his stride. This manœuvre can be practised over the cross-bar of the goal. Players line up with a ball each on the twenty-five line, run straight towards the goal, and when about 6 yards away make a short punt over the bar, catch the ball as it comes down on the other side, and score an imaginary " try " over the dead-ball line. It is only fair to warn the beginner, however, that such an exercise is much easier said than done.

Except for sheer individual perseverance, there is little that can be done in the way of minor games to improve a player's accuracy in punting. One Rugger school has made an attempt to deal with this problem by inserting a single tall goal-post into the ground in one corner of the playing-field, with concentric circles drawn round it at 20, 25, 30, 35, and 40 yards radius. Half a dozen boys spread out round one of the circles, and, with two or three balls in action, try to hit the post with punts; as soon as a hit is registered from the 20-yard circle, all the boys move out to the 25-yard ring, and start again from there. The difficulty about such a practice is that concentrated punting is very tiring, and care must be taken not to overstrain the thigh muscles. In fact, the motto for punting practice should be " a little and often ".

The last type of kick which the keen Rugger player can practise is the ordinary place-kick. Fortunately, this lends itself to solo practice, and the correct procedure has already been fully explained in Chapter IV under the heading of " Kicking ".

D. Dribbling

There is no denying the fact that a certain amount of luck is required to make a long and successful dribble with a Rugger ball; it could not very well be otherwise with an oval-shaped ball. But by constant practice, this element of luck can be reduced to a minimum, as the player succeeds in obtaining more and more control over the ball as it gradually becomes tamed from the awkwardly rolling and elusive egg stage to the seemingly tied-to-the-bootlace stage. Of course, there is a wide gap between the two extremes of the beginner and the international; nevertheless, here to follow are a few exercises designed to narrow that gap.

One simple dribbling drill is for four players to queue up behind each other a yard or two apart. A, E, and H, the leaders of three teams, begin a dribble down the field. The coach sounds his whistle every few seconds, and at the first blow, A, E, and H fall back to the end of the queue for B, F, and I to carrying on dribbling; at the next

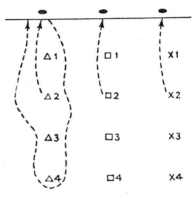

whistle, they in turn withdraw in favour of C, G, and J. The players must be taught the fundamental principles of dribbling a Rugger ball before the exercise begins, but they will quickly learn for themselves the essential differences between keeping the ball close and pure " kick and rush ". A variation which is useful for small spaces is to have, say, three teams of four in lines about 6 yards apart, with a ball on the ground in front of each team. In order to encourage quickness of thought and action, the coach calls out a number, say " No. 2 ", and immediately the three players standing second in their lines dash out to the ball in front of their team, turn and dribble it round the rest of their team, and so back to the front, where the winner is the one who scores a " try " first. The coach might then call " No. 4 ", and so on until all have had a turn or two.

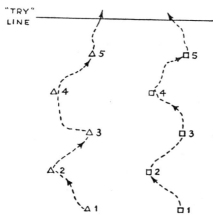

These minor team games are very popular with small boys, and another good way to teach dribbling is a simple zig-zag relay. Teams of five take up their positions as in the diagram, and when the coach sounds his whistle, No. 1 dribbles his Rugger ball to No. 2, who dribbles it to No. 3, and so on, until the last member of the team has again to try to beat his opponents by touching down first for an imaginary " try ".

" Rugby Wheel " is another very good minor

team game. Three teams of four players in each line up along radii of an 8- or 10-yard circle, all facing, say, in an anti-clockwise direction. At the whistle, all three of the outside players begin to dribble a Rugger ball round the outside of the circle. When each No. 1 gets back to his original

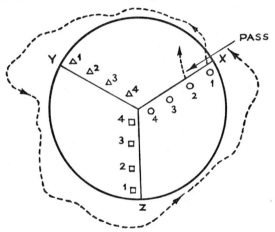

starting-point at X, Y, and Z, he picks up the ball and gives a pass to his No. 2, who in turn dribbles round and hands on to No. 3. The first No. 1 to receive the ball again from his No. 4 is the winner.

E. Passing

Whereas dribbling a Rugger ball is a somewhat uncertain factor, and therefore does not lend itself easily to competitive team games, passing the ball from one player to another can—and should—be a

much more accurate business. In the early stages
it does not matter so much about the ball being
thrown forward, but later on it is better to concentrate on those minor games in which all passing
conforms to the rules of the major game itself.
" Passing Spry " is a useful starting point, mainly
to teach handling and to get the general " feel "
of a Rugger ball.

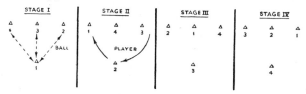

If four players make a team, the principle is that
No. 1 goes out in front, passes the ball to each of
his three team-mates in turn, and then joins the
left of the line while No. 2 runs out in front to
carry out the same sequence. Thus all four players
occupy every position in turn, and in order to
speed things up, as many teams as possible compete
against each other. A variation of this spry is to
have three pairs of players trotting round a small
circle of about 5 yards radius, each pair having one
Rugger ball between them. The coach blows his
whistle every few seconds, and on each occasion the
ball is passed across the circle to the partners. By
changing every now and then from clockwise to
anti-clockwise running, passes can be practised both
to right and to left.

" Wandering Ball " is another passing game

played round a circle, this time of about 6 yards radius. The players, any reasonable number, face *outwards* from the centre, so that every pass is a backward one. One " interceptor " rushes about trying to obtain possession of the ball as each player passes it to the neighbour on his left or his right. Once the interceptor succeeds, the player who gave the last pass takes his place, and the game goes on with a new interceptor.

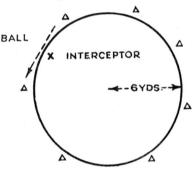

Here is another simple passing relay race. Four or five members of a team stand close behind each other, while their leader with a Rugger ball stands 6 yards away in front of the line. As soon as the whistle goes, each leader passes the ball to his No. 1, who catches it, returns it, and at once sits down out of the way. The leader then passes over No. 1 to No. 2, who catches, passes back, and sits down; and so on. " Pass and Kneel " relay is a similar variation. If it is required to introduce passing on the run, a " zig-zag pass relay " can be played. It is similar to the zig-zag dribbling game already described, except that the ball is carried instead of dribbled; consequently it is much faster. Also each player must run *beyond* the receiver in order to pass backward to his colleague.

Probably the best game of all for developing and improving passing is " Rugby Touch ". There are several varieties of this jolly and fast game, but the general principle is that as soon as a player is touched when he is in possession of the ball, he must immediately pass. Almost any number of players can join in, and the field varies in size accordingly. It is an excellent game for teaching players to pass ahead of a colleague and to run into empty spaces, two fundamental tactical moves in the major game itself.

F. Combined Skills

In recent years, quite a few team games have been devised to help in the training of a group of club members before, or instead of, an ordinary Rugger practice. Some of them, which combine a number of different skills, are given below.

A good comprehensive relay race which requires only a little preparation is illustrated in the above diagram. The first player of each team has a

Rugger ball, and as soon as the coach sounds his
whistle, he runs up to the line, makes a short punt
ahead, catches the ball, runs to a hoop or a circle
marked out on the ground, drops the ball and
begins to dribble between two flags 6 feet apart,
picks up the ball again, turns and swerves back
through a number of flags or sticks before handing
on to the second member of his team, who goes
through the same procedure. If you make a poor
show of such a relay at the first attempt, do not
despair, because once you have got the idea, progress will be rapid; and with two or three other
teams competing alongside, such a comprehensive
relay can be most exciting.

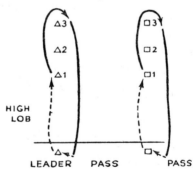

A simpler relay, very useful for forwards, can be
played when the members of a team line up close
behind each other, while the leader with a Rugger
ball stands behind a line 10 yards away. At the
sound of the whistle, the leader lobs a high pass,
as in a line-out, to his No. 1, who jumps for the

ball, catches it, races round his own team, and so back *beyond* his leader before giving him a backward pass. All the team repeat this simple manœuvre, trying to carry it out quicker than their opposing teams.

A simple little exercise to improve dribbling and catching is one which any keen player can enjoy with a friend. The two players stand behind lines drawn 10 yards apart; A lobs a high pass to B, who leaps up to catch the ball and releases it immediately to start a dribble towards A's line. As soon as he has crossed this, B picks up the ball and lobs it high above A, who in the meantime has also crossed over; A catches it, dribbles across, and lobs to B. Five minutes of this simple but exhilarating practice really does improve your catching and dribbling. An alternative version of this " lob, catch, dribble, and cross " exercise is for each player to do a short punt across the 10-yard interval between the lines instead of a high lob. Similarly, if more room is available, the two players can go out on to a field; A makes a short punt ahead, catches it, dribbles 5 yards, picks up on the run, and passes back to B, who is following up. B then goes through the same motions.

" Rugger Volley Ball " is an enjoyable indoor or outdoor game for two, four, or six players. All that is required is a small court marked out on the floor about the size of a badminton court and a high net or rope about 7 feet 6 inches above the ground. The players catch and immediately throw

back the Rugger ball, trying to make it touch the
ground before their opponents can catch it; 9, 15,
or 21 points generally count as game. It is obviously a useful practice to teach players to catch a
ball, and as it is permissible to spin it both endways
and sideways, it is essential to keep your eyes on the
ball the whole time.

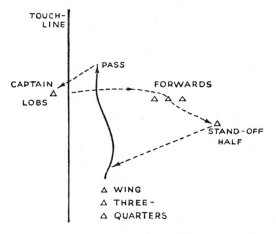

A minor practice which combines a number of
the features of an ordinary Rugger game can be
worked out between one or two forwards, a stand-off
half, and some wing three-quarters. A captain or
leader lobs the ball in from the touch-line as in a
normal game, a forward catches it, pivots round in
mid-air, and passes to his stand-off half some 10
yards away; he in turn throws out a long pass to
the first of the wing three-quarters, who races along

the touch-line beyond his captain before passing back to him. The captain again lobs the ball in, and the movement is repeated. With two or three wingers, the exercise can continue without any waste of time. It should be emphasised that this *is* an exercise, and not a movement to be encouraged during actual match-play.

The many drills and exercises which have been enumerated in this chapter by no means exhaust the possibilities of " purposeful minor team games ". In fact, the keen learner will probably have thought of a few variations and improvements even as he has been reading. Yet just a word of warning is necessary. No good coach or captain will keep his players hard at these exercises for long; they are only a means to an end, and the end is the game of Rugger itself. Minor games administered in small doses are excellent stimulants, but it should always be remembered that their main purpose is the strengthening of weaknesses and not an alternative for the real thing.

CHAPTER VI

FORWARD PLAY

THERE is an old-fashioned idea in British Rugby that the forward is a great hulking fellow, a " muddied oaf" who is all brawn and no brain; that his main, almost his only, function is to shove hard and battle for the ball in order to give it to his three-quarters, who then score tries. This notion is now very much out of date, as Dominions' teams, particularly, have shown us. The modern forward has to be an intelligent all-round performer, who must be ready to play his part in defence and attack, both in the " tight " and in the " open ". Once you have decided to be a forward, there comes the question as to which position in the pack you are best fitted for. As shown in the following diagram, forwards are named according to their positions in a set scrum:

```
T |           FRONT        HOOKER          FRONT
O |           ROW    o        o         o   ROW
U |           FORWARD                        FORWARD
C |
H |
  |
L |                        o         o    SECOND ROW FORWARDS
I |
N |
E |
  |
  |        WING FORWARD o              o WING FORWARD
  |        BLIND SIDE        o LOCK      OPEN SIDE
```

First of all, it is necessary to issue a warning against too much specialisation. Try to be a *forward*, not merely a wing forward, or a second-row forward, or a lock. There are two good reasons for this. First, the more you widen your experience of the game, the better you play in any one position; this principle extends beyond the scrum, and it is an excellent thing for a forward to have to play, for example, at scrum-half occasionally, so that he can see the pack from a fresh point of view. Second, if you are a specialist, it reduces your chances of getting into a side; for example, if you join the Services and you tell your Sports Officer that you are a second-row forward, you may not stand a chance of a place, for he may already have a couple of internationals in the second row! Call yourself a forward, however, and your chances are very much better.

Nevertheless, especially in the higher flights of Rugger, some players are physically better fitted than others for the different positions in the pack. The front-row men, for example, need plenty of weight, but are best short and stocky, as this will help them to pack lower than the opposition. The second-row men, too, must be strongly built, for they provide a great deal of the shove, and they must also be capable of transmitting the push from the back-row forwards. Unlike the front row, however, it is an advantage if they are tall, as this helps considerably in the line-out. The lock must be powerfully built, too, for he assists a good deal in holding the whole scrum together. So far as the wing forwards are concerned, weight is less important than speed and an all-round ability at the game.

The Kick-off

In considering a forward's job, let us start at the beginning of a game—with the kick-off. Many sides do not realise the importance of going all out from the start. This, the kick-off, is the moment to go hell-for-leather, to try to rock the opposition back on its heels, and to assert your will to win. If it is your kick-off and your kicker decides to kick left, your forwards should fan out towards the left touch-line. They should all keep behind the kicker —or they will be off-side and a " scrum-back " will be given on the centre spot—and run up with him. Each forward should go as hard as he can and should try to put down the opponent who catches the ball. Most of the forwards should converge on him, to be ready to form a loose scrum if he should be tackled in possession, but—and this applies particularly to the forwards nearest the kicker—some should watch for any attempt to start a passing movement. If, for example, the ball is fielded and passed inwards towards the centre of the field, then the slower forwards should fan out and try to smother the opposition. If it is your opponents' kick-off, the defending forwards should form up something like this :

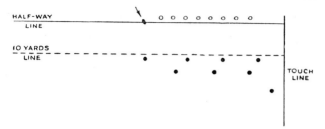

Watch carefully for a " wrong 'un ".   Sometimes
a kicker will spread out all his forwards on his left
and then kick-off towards the right, hoping that
his own fast-moving backs—forewarned of the
manœuvre—may seize possession and outflank the
defending forwards.   In defence, if you are able to
catch the ball, the usual thing is to kick for touch,
and so gain a footing in the enemy half right away.
Be careful, though, not to have your kick charged
down; rather than that, it is better to " die with
it ", in other words, hang on to the ball until you
are finally grounded, and so give your fellow forwards a chance to pack round and form a loose
scrum.   Alternatively—and especially if you field
the ball well out from touch—you can run inwards,
pass towards the centre of the field, and start an
attacking movement.

The Set Scrum

Let us now suppose that, in trying to catch that
ball from the kick-off, greasy perhaps and swirling
about in the wind, you knock it on.   The whistle
goes for a set scrum, for a set scrum is the main

way of re-starting the game after a minor infringement of the rules, giving each side an almost equal
chance of obtaining possession of the ball. There
are usually eight forwards on each side, and they
normally arrange themselves in one of these two
formations :

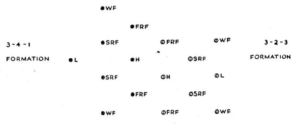

In each front row there are three forwards, of
whom the middle one is the hooker. Let us
imagine, for the moment, that you are the hooker.
You place one arm round the neck of the front-
row forward on either side of you, while they wrap
their inside arms round your waist. You then all
three " bind " together. You stand opposite the
opposing hooker and, bending down, shove your
head between him and one of his front-row forwards; you go either side of him, as we shall see
later. We have now laid the foundations of the set
scrum, with the two front rows down and forming
a sort of arch between them.

Next it is the turn of the second rows; these
forwards first bind tightly together by wrapping

their inside arms firmly round one another's waists.
They then bend down and stick their heads in the
gaps between the behinds of the front-row men.
Next the forward known as the " lock " places his
head between the behinds of the second-row men;
and finally the two wing forwards—so called because
they form the " wings " of the scrum—get down and
shove against the outside buttocks of the second-
row men in the 3–2–3 formation and on the front-
row men in the 3–4–1 formation. So the scrum is
formed. The scrum-half then puts the ball in the
arch mid-way between the two hookers, while the
two packs are shoving to try to gain the advantage
and so assist their hooker to hook the ball back
through their own scrum and so ultimately to their
own three-quarters.

So much for the set scrum in general terms. Now
let us look at it a little more closely and consider
what points the forwards must bear in mind if the
scrum as a whole is to be a good one. In the first
place, every man must see to it that he is in such a
position as will enable him to shove hard himself
and also communicate the shove of those behind.
For this reason, everyone must pack *low*. The
front-row men should always try to pack a little
lower than their opponents, for this will help
enormously in obtaining that extra bit of shove
which gives the hooker the advantage. Similarly,
the second-row forwards and the lock must be careful to get their shoulders underneath the curve of
the buttocks of the men in front. If they fail to

do this and then try to shove, they will naturally slide up their backs and the shove will not be communicated to the front row where it is wanted.

It is also vital that every player should square his shoulders and *hollow his back*. Your back, like a pen-knife, will bend one way but not the other, and if you have your back hollowed no amount of pushing from behind can make you crumple. If it is ever so slightly arched, however, it will buckle upwards when the shove comes through. Sometimes when the second row shove hard and low, you will notice a front-row man's seat hoisted ignominiously into the air if he is pushing with an arched back, and the scrum collapses!

The next essential is that every player must have his feet in the correct position. Let us take the left front-row forward first; he should have his left foot forward and well bent, and his right foot back almost behind his left. In this way he will leave the widest possible channel for the ball to travel back through the scrum, and, in addition, the placing of this rear foot a little outward from the centre of the scrum causes him to shove slightly inwards, thus helping to bind the scrum together. The second-row forwards should have their outside feet in front and inside feet back, again to form a kind of corridor down the middle back to the scrum-half. The lock should have both feet back and apart. All the forwards must take great care to keep their feet out of the way of the ball as it skids back through the scrum; if it should stick, they should push it on its way firmly but gently, and certainly not so hard that the scrum-half cannot gather it cleanly as it emerges.

Finally, we come to the shove itself. A good tip here is to get down as quickly as possible; the side first down often wins the scrum. Do not, as some teams do, form your scrums a yard or two apart and then crash in a head-on collision. At worst it can be dangerous, at best it is very unpleasant, and the object of a game of Rugby is to enjoy yourself! But it *is* worth while fighting for the " loose head ". Look for a moment at this simple diagram:

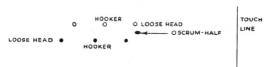

It shows both front rows down, and you can see that one forward on each side does not have his head wedged between two opponents—his head is " loose ". Now the scrum-half usually puts the ball in from the side on which his own team has the loose head, as the White scrum-half is doing in the diagram. It is obvious that by doing this the ball comes to the White hooker first. In order, however, to try to even out this advantage of the loose head the law has recently been amended to allow the hooker to strike with his foot nearer the tight head. What may not be quite so obvious to a beginner is that it is always an advantage to have the loose head nearest to the touch-line so that the scrum-half puts the ball in from that side, and so, when it is heeled, he is facing the centre of the field and can set his three-quarters moving without having to turn round at the base of the scrum.   Here are the two possibilities:

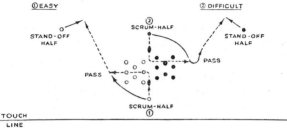

Once down, do not waste your energy on pushing for all you are worth.   If you have ever watched a tug-of-war team, you have probably noticed that each man does not jerk away at the rope for the whole time; he digs his heels in and " holds ", until at a signal from the trainer the whole team gives a *concerted* heave and gets the opposing team on the move.   The same principle is used in Rugby scrummage work.   As you wait for the ball to come in, hold your opponents' shove, keeping your knees slightly bent; then the scrum-half will say " Coming in left (or right).   Now ! "   As he calls out " Now ", everyone in the pack straightens his knees, the whole eight gives a concerted heave, and the opposition recoils, perhaps only a foot or so, but just enough to give your hooker the advantage.   It is a good plan for the front-row forwards, if they are pushing lower than their opponents, to push *upwards* as well

as forwards; this helps to disorganise the other
scrum at the vital moment.

Hooking

Let us assume, then, that your eight have won
the shoving battle. It is now up to your hooker to
make use of his advantage. He should be packing
low and slightly slewed round in the direction from
which the ball is to come in, and his eyes should
be fixed on the ball in the hands of the scrum-half.
As the laws stand at present, he must hook the ball
with the foot farthest from the loose-head side or
nearest to the tight-head side. He must be careful,
however, not to raise his foot before the ball has left
the hands of the scrum-half.

Yet the hooker is not the only player who may
hook the ball from a set scrum. The front-row
forwards, by a recent amendment to the laws, may
follow in the ball with their outside feet and help
to get the ball back. The ball, we imagined, comes
in on the hooker's left. In that case, the front-row
man on the left follows the ball in with his left foot
and may be able to get the ball back if, as often
happens, the ball rebounds off the hooker's boot.
If both hookers miss the ball, then the front-row
forward on the *right* has a chance to hook it.

Formations

We saw that there are two common formations
for set scrums, known usually as packing 3–2–3

and 3-4-1. The advantage of the 3-2-3 method
is that it makes fuller use of the pack's weight,
since the total shove is concentrated in a narrower
part. The advantages of the 3-4-1 method are
that your wing forwards are a foot or two nearer
to their opponents and so can attack them a shade
more quickly; at the same time, your scrum is
wider and gives more protection to your own
scrum-half. It is all a matter of taste and tactics,
but a guiding principle might be that you should
pack 3-4-1 when you have a considerable superiority
in weight, otherwise you should stick to the more
orthodox 3-2-3 formation.

Holding the Ball in the Scrum—Wheeling

We have seen that the primary object in the
scrum is to obtain possession of the ball, and this
usually aims at hooking it through to the scrum-
half at the base. Sometimes, however, it is better
to hold the ball in the scrum. For instance, if you
obtain a scrum within a few yards of your opponents'
line—and especially if it is wet and the backs find
handling difficult—there is no reason why you
should not hook the ball into the middle of your
scrum and then, taking the ball with you, shove
your opponents back over their own line. Once
there, you have only to fall on the ball for a try.
This, incidentally, is the one occasion when it is
permissible to handle the ball in the scrum. Again,
from a scrum near your own line, it is sometimes
better not to hook a slippery ball straight back to

your scrum-half, because if one of the halves fumbles it, the opposing wing forwards might sweep round the scrum, obtain possession and score. It was to counter this manœuvre near the goal-line that the " wheel " was invented. Let us imagine you are awarded a scrum near your own line and 10 yards in from the right-hand touch-line. If your hooker wins the battle for the ball, the back-row forwards do not allow the ball to pass through; they hold it instead. Then, with the forwards on the left giving ground slightly and those on the right shoving extra hard, the whole scrum is slewed round *towards touch*. When about half-way round, the back-row forwards break away with the ball at their feet, and sweep down the field parallel to the touch-line. It is essential to wheel towards touch, because if you wheel to the middle of the field, one of the forwards may kick the ball just too far ahead, and thus make a present of it to the opposition in the open.

There is to-day a school of thought which holds that the wheel is out of date, because an opposing wing forward has only to dive over the ball, putting his body between it and the breaking forwards, and *his* side can then secure a quick heel from a loose scrum. So far as international Rugby is concerned, there may be considerable truth in this, but in club and school games, where the ball is more likely to stick on its journey through the scrum and the scrum-half more likely to fumble, it is as dangerous as ever it was to heel a greasy ball on your own line, and for that reason the wheel is well worth practising.

The Break-up from the Scrum : Attack

In nine scrums out of ten, then, your primary job as a pack is to get the ball back to your three-quarters as quickly as possible; but if you succeed in this, do not be content to rest on your oars and leave it to the outsides. You must now help them to carry on the good work. Perhaps, for example, your backs are being marked so closely that they are making little headway with the ball once they have it. Your stand-off half, noticing this, might decide to " sell a dummy " to his opposite number and cut back towards the scrum, thus altering the direction of attack and catching the opposition on the wrong foot. The open-side wing forward and the lock in that case should be up for his pass, and if the other forwards break quickly they should be in position for a short-passing, attacking movement.

Or perhaps the ball may be swung quickly out to the far wing three-quarter; he makes as much headway as he can and then, before he is tackled, he cross kicks ahead of his forwards, who should be just behind him—and therefore on-side—and spread out ready to gather such a kick. This manœuvre is particularly effective when the opposing forwards have been drawn across the field to tackle your backs. It calls for accurate kicking by the wing, who must drop the ball just so far ahead of his forwards that they can reach it racing at full

speed. It is also a question of intelligent anticipation by the forwards.

Apart from these two specific manœuvres, the
forwards—and particularly the back-row and sometimes the loose-head front-row forward—should
always break quickly and come up in support of
their three-quarters ready to join in a movement or
to snap up a dropped pass. It is usually best for a
blind-side wing forward to go up his own side of the
scrum and then move across towards the centre of the
field, keeping just on-side. He will then find that
he sometimes meets an opposing centre cutting
back in search of an opening.

The Break-up from the Scrum : Defence

When the opposing hooker wins the ball, you, as
forwards, must not regard your job as temporarily
finished; you must help your outsides in defence.
Someone in your pack—the hooker or the leader,
or possibly the scrum-half—should call out clearly
" Break ", so that the forwards with their heads
down who are unable to see what happens to the
ball will know what to do at the earliest possible
moment.

It is important to arrange beforehand what job
each forward is going to do in defence when breaking up from a scrum. Most scrums work in some
such fashion as is illustrated in the diagram below.
Whites are attacking, having won the ball from a
scrum, and their outsides are lined well back so as
to be able to take their passes running fast. The

Black three-quarters, on the other hand, are lying well up, so as to get as near as possible to their opponents to tackle them. The White scrum-half has put the ball in on the loose-head side, and his hooker has hooked it; the scrum-half dashes round to the base of his scrum to fling the ball out ahead of his waiting stand-off half. Now study the diagram carefully to see what action the individual Black forwards should take.

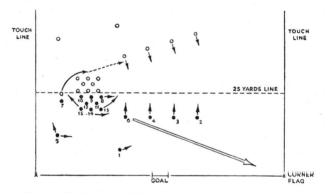

First of all, the blind-side wing forward (15) should go round the scrum and try to collar the opposing scrum-half and smother him before he can pass out to his stand-off. This is the most effective way of stifling an attack—before it starts! But he must take great care not to be off-side; on his own twenty-five line that would usually mean losing three points at once. If he cannot get round quickly enough—and it must be realised that a good scrum-half behind a clean-heeling pack of

forwards will usually evade him—he must not forget
his general responsibility for defence on the blind
side of the scrum, and so he must keep a weather
eye on the White right-wing three-quarter.

Secondly, the open-side wing forward (13) should
aim to tackle the opposing stand-off half. In many
ways the stand-off is the pivot of the attack; he
often decides its speed and direction, and if he
manages to cut through on his own, it is not far to
the line. It is essential, then, to put this dangerous
man down and to tackle him before he gets his line
moving; in consequence, two players, the wing
forward (13) and the stand-off half (6), share the
responsibility of dealing with him. If the White
stand-off passes early, then the Black open-side wing
forward can go after the right centre, and so across
the line. It is not unknown, in fact, for a wing
forward to race across the width of the field as the
ball is passed from man to man and then finally
to tackle the wing three-quarter !

As soon as he hears the word " Break ", then,
the open-side wing forward makes for the opposing
stand-off half. Supposing, however, that the opposing scrum-half does not pass the ball out, but cuts
inside the quick-breaking wing forward. In that
case, it is the job of the lock (14) to get his head
up quickly and smother the scrum-half before he
can do any more damage. The burden of defence
from the set scrums naturally falls on the back row,
who can be in action first, but that by no means
implies that the second and front rows will take no

part. It is no use those players heading straight for any opponent who happens to have the ball; what they must do is to steer a course which will head off the attack, and a good general rule for them is to make for the corner-flag as shown by the thick arrow in the diagram.

Loose Scrums

A set scrum occurs after an infringement of the laws; the whistle blows, there is a pause in the game, and all the players have time to take up their positions. Forwards get into their own niches in the scrum, stand-off half and three-quarters align themselves opposite to the men they have to mark, and everything is comparatively formal and organised.

A loose scrum is very different; there is no break in the game. Perhaps a three-quarter has been tackled and the ball " sticks " on the ground somewhere in the heap of tackler and tackled; or perhaps the forwards have been dribbling and a scrum-half has fallen on the ball to check their advance. Your job, then, as a forward, is to get the ball moving again and carry on the interrupted attack at the earliest possible moment. As you come up to the ball, bind quickly with the man next to you, get your head well down, walk over the ball and hook it back. Do not worry about the set-scrum order; just pack down in the order you come up, but the wing forwards should still take care to guard their respective sides, especially near their

own line. Every forward must be in and packing;
there is nothing more annoying for a scrum-half
than to have forwards getting in his way by loafing
about a yard or so away from the scrum. Every
forward, too, must keep his eyes on the ball and
take good care to keep his feet out of the way as
the ball comes back.

Perhaps nothing distinguishes a good pack from
a bad one more than the ability to form good loose
scrums. In the set scrums every forward knows his
job; he knows where to pack and how, and he
knows that it is essential for him to be there. It is
very much more difficult to train a pack to put all
their energy into a loose scrum. Yet a moment's
thought will show that success in loose scrums is
far more important than success in set scrums.
One famous stand-off half has even gone so far as
to say that a heel in the loose is worth ten in the
tight. Why is this? Let us suppose an enemy
centre three-quarter has been tackled in possession
by one of your wing forwards. Down they go in a
heap; a loose scrum forms like lightning, and the
ball is whipped out on your side. Your team is
now in a much more dangerous attacking position
than it would be after a quick heel from a set
scrum, because that enemy centre three-quarter is
still at the bottom of the heap! Your backs, as
they sweep forward in attack, should therefore have
a man over, so that the wing three-quarter should
have a clear run with only the full-back to beat.
Before a set scrum, then, the opposition has a few

vital moments in which to reorganise, but before a loose scrum there is no pause in the game, and you can be over their line before they have time to repair the holes in their defences.

The Line-out

When the ball goes out into touch, play is restarted by means of a line-out. The touch judge holds his flag up in one hand and points with the other to the side which is entitled to the throw-in.

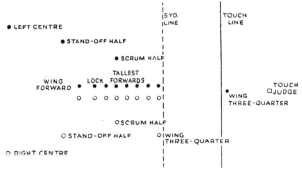

Exactly opposite to the touch judge and at a minimum distance of 5 yards out from touch, the forwards form two parallel lines at right angles to the touch-line. The wing three-quarter then throws the ball in between these two lines, while the forwards jump and try to secure possession of the ball.

Positions in the Line-out

It is advisable at the outset to have a provisional order for standing in the line-out. As will be seen from the above diagram, the wing forwards and the lock will normally be at the back of the line, because from there they are best able to attack the opposing stand-off half and centres; they are also nearest to the middle of the field, where most danger will threaten. Some sides, however, prefer to keep one wing forward near the front of the line-out, so that if a loose scrum results, there will be a wing forward on each flank of it. The tallest forwards are best grouped about the middle of the line, say numbers 3, 4, and 5 from the front; numbers 1 and 2, who rarely get the ball, will be the shorter ones. This order, however, should be only provisional and able to be changed according to circumstances. If your opponents have a particularly tall and skilful line-out player, their wingers will try to throw the ball to him; therefore your tallest and strongest forward must be told to mark him. If it is *your* throw-in, on the other hand, then your own expert must try to get unmarked or at least to stand opposite someone smaller and lighter than himself. In any case, mark a man, particularly when it is your opponents' throw-in; be very determined about this, and what-ever happens do not allow your opposite number to break away with the ball.

Tactics at the Line-out

The possible tactics at the line-out are so varied and depend on so many factors—the score, the effectiveness of your outsides compared with your opponents, the state of the ground, and the wind—that what to do at each line-out can only be decided

E

on the spot. This is a decision which the leader of the forwards must always make at the time, and all that can be done here is to give some general considerations for him to work on.

(a) *Attack from the Line-out.* If you feel that you are in an attacking position, you will try to get the ball to your three-quarters, just as you do from a set scrum. The quickest way to do this is to jump for the ball, catch it, and have it out to the stand-off half as quickly as possible, so that he can get his line moving. Yet there are a few important points to note in connection with this, the simplest form of attacking movement from the line-out. For instance, it is of little use trying it unless the ball falls in the back half of the line, because if it falls in the front half, the opposing wing forwards at the back will be smothering your stand-off half and centres before they can get on the move.

Let us suppose that you are No. 6 in a line-out, and you can see that the ball is going to drop near you. It is a good thing to stand slightly behind the man you are marking and then, as the ball falls, to jump upwards and forwards with hands outstretched to catch the ball. This sounds easy enough, but if you are tired, it takes great will-power to make yourself jump clear of the ground time after time to reach for the ball; moreover, it takes considerable skill to judge the best moment to jump. Note that you should *catch* the ball; you do not knock it back. It is true that a recent Australian touring side knocked the ball back from the line-out with great success, but they practised it as a team system, and one forward, as soon as the ball was thrown in, always dropped back to help the scrum-half in defence. So, unless it is deliberate team policy, the golden rule still stands— never knock back.

Imagine, then, that you have leapt and caught the ball at No. 6. To get the ball to the backs as quickly as possible, you should slew round towards your own goal-line and pass the ball from the over-head position to the scrum-half, or better still if you can manage it to the stand-off half. Now notice that this is a good manœuvre only if you get the ball back *quickly*. If there is any delay, if you fumble with the ball for a moment, the opposing forwards will be through and on to your halves before they can start a movement. If you fumble, then, hang on to the ball, and try to barge through instead.

The great disadvantage of this method of attack from the line-out is the danger that your pass might go astray or that the half-back might fumble and allow the opposing forwards to break through and sweep away with the ball. So we need another method of getting the ball back to the three-quarters from the line-out, if possible one which will engage the whole opposing pack so that they are not free to break through on to your halves. The way to do this is to catch the ball as before, bring it down to your feet, and heel. Every man in the line-out, moving very quickly, must form a scrum, with the player who catches the ball in the position of hooker. The opposition is bound to form a loose scrum to hold your formation. The man with the ball then drops it at his feet and heels it to the waiting scrum-half; he must not throw it through his own legs. This method may seem slower, but it is safer, especially with a wet ball, and it should be used much more widely by club sides, most of which try far too often to pass straight back from the line-out.

A third way of getting the ball back to your out-sides is to form a medium line—that is, not a long line or a bunch—and then for the player who catches the ball to barge through as far as he can, with his team-mates forming a loose scrum on him. In that way they might carry it some distance or—particularly if the ball is greasy—dribble it as a pack; then, when they are stopped, they heel it quickly to the waiting scrum-half. This method also engages the opposing forwards, and might even draw an opposing half-back to fall on the ball or tackle, so that your backs, when they receive the ball, might be a man over.

Finally, the most obvious way to attack from the line-out is to break clean through it. A good method of doing this is to jump for the ball, catch it, turn towards your halves as if you are about to throw it to one of them, but at the last moment bring the ball down into your stomach, stick your behind out like a battering ram, and go through the opposing line backwards. You must not begin

your barge before the ball reaches you; the referee
will award a penalty-kick against you if you take the
ball as you fall through between two opponents.
This is called "charging in the line-out", and
referees are becoming more and more strict in
checking it. Once you are clear, make for the line
if you are near enough, but look out for your own
forwards coming through in support. If you are in
your own half, and not likely to get far along the
touch-line, try to work in towards mid-field and
then get the ball to your three-quarters.

So much for the question of attack from the line-
out. It may all sound rather complicated, but it
will simplify things if you remember that in the
first instance you always do the same thing—jump
for the ball and catch it if it drops near enough to
you. If it goes over your head or is obviously
dropping short of you, run and pack round the
player with the ball.

(b) *Defence at the Line-out.* If your opponents
obtain possession of the ball at a line-out, you
must try to reduce their advantage to a minimum.
If the particular man you are marking catches the
ball, there are several things you can do to frustrate
him. You can tackle him, ball and all, with a
bear-hug, so that he can neither pass nor heel. If
he is much bigger and stronger than you are, you
can tackle him by the ankles and up-end him the
moment he catches the ball. Or finally—and
especially if you stand slightly behind him—you
can tap his arms smartly immediately he has the

ball in his possession and so make him drop it. Whichever way you do it, the great thing is—stop your man. As in attack, if an opponent gets the ball, you must gather round and support your colleague who has tackled him, thus making a break-through as difficult as possible.

Finally, there is one line-out formation which is really always defensive in the sense that your aim is to regain lost ground rather than begin a movement to score. This is the " bunch-and-take " method, which should almost invariably be used in your own twenty-five, and often in your own half, especially when the ball is greasy. In this formation the two packs of forwards stand in two bunches just over the 5-yard line. The object is to secure possession of the ball and take it away down the touch-line, either by supporting with all available weight the man with the ball or by a combined dribbling effort. With such bunches you can often work your way a few yards at a time down a touch-line into safer territory.

Forwards in Attack

We have already seen how forwards can be effective in attack by backing up their own three-quarters, and it cannot be emphasised too frequently that in modern Rugby every forward should keep going the whole time. There are two main ways, however, in which forwards can attack as a pack. The first is by short inter-passing, an art which the New Zealanders perfected, and at which Dominion teams still surpass the Home Countries. For this method of attack, the forwards do not string out at maximum effective passing distance. Instead, they advance in a mass, not merely a line, a few yards apart, whipping the ball from one to the other, sometimes even passing straight backwards and altering the direction of attack. There should be *eight* forwards there, not merely the keenest four or five, and if they keep going all out, it is very hard to stop them.

Secondly, there is the dribble, a deadly method of attack when the ground is wet, the ball greasy, and handling difficult. We have already considered the art of dribbling in Chapter IV, but when you are working as a pack, there are a few more points to be borne in mind. The player with the ball at his feet must be ahead of the rest, so that everybody is on-side. The ball may veer off to right or left; for this reason, the man with the ball should have a forward a few yards on either side of him and slightly behind him. Again, the dribbler may over-run the ball, so you must have another forward backing up about 3 yards behind him. The skeleton of a simple dribbling formation, then, is as follows:

DIRECTION OF DRIBBLE

If the other four forwards are up as well, their best formation is probably one more on each wing

and two more in the rear. The whole object is to
keep the dribble going; and the first thing likely
to stop it is the ball itself, for that odd-shaped piece
of inflated leather is terribly hard to control. Let
us suppose that the ball veers away to your right
as you are dribbling; look at these diagrams to
see what happens to each of the four forwards
concerned:

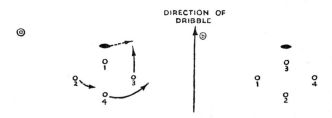

In (a), No. 1 loses the ball to his right. No. 3
takes on and advances a little ahead of the others;
No. 4 comes up on his right, and No. 2 drops
back into the rear position. The result is that the
dribble continues as in formation (b).

Similarly, if you are dribbling and you over-
step the ball, you must get out of the way as quickly
as possible. Look at the two simple diagrams
below. In (a) we will suppose that No. 1 over-
runs the ball. He may get clear to the left and
drop into No. 2's position. No. 4 will advance and
take the ball on, while No. 2 will drop back to the
rear. The movement will then continue as in the
new formation (b).

With more forwards up, others may move naturally into the right positions; but remember that, however you do it, you must always have at least one player on each side of and slightly behind the dribbler, and one bringing up the rear.

If you manage to keep possession of the ball in spite of the difficulties inherent in controlling an oval ball at speed, you might lose it by " enemy action ". There are two main ways in which an

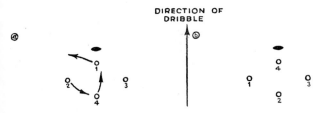

opponent can stop a concerted dribble. If he is fast and a sure handler, he might race across your advancing front, snap up the ball, and kick for touch. As an alternative, he might fall on it. To guard against the first manœuvre, you must keep the ball *close* in a dribble, not more than a yard or two from your feet. It may be necessary to sacrifice a certain amount of speed to do this, but it is worth it. To foil the man trying to fall on the ball is a more difficult problem, but it can be done by tapping the ball sideways to a colleague, or if the player falling is the last line of defence, by kicking the ball past him and racing for the touch-down. If he does fall on the ball successfully, you may, if you are quick, be able to step over him, free the ball, and carry on the dribble; but it is often better, at such a stage, to form a loose scrum, heel, and get the three-quarters moving.

The Leader of the Forwards

No chapter on Forward Play would be complete without a reference to that most important person—the leader of the pack. It is only if he does his job really well that eight individuals can be welded into an efficient scrum. The forwards can be led from any position in the pack, although a wing forward is perhaps the least suitable, as he is so often out and away on his own. The pack leader is to the forwards what the captain is to the whole side. He—and he only on the field of play—should take charge of his eight. He should see that they are properly arranged for the kick-off. He must make sure that they are packing well in the set scrums, and he should tell them, in doubtful cases, whether they want a " quick heel " or a " wheel and take ". He should also shout " Break "—or detail someone else to do so—whenever the ball is lost.

In the line-out, as we have seen, the leader, having regard to the state of the game, must decide whether the condition of the ground, the wind, and similar factors require him to call " Long line and back it ", or " Bunch and take ", or " Take until you're stopped, then back it ", and so on. He thus lays down the policy in every line-out, but he must realise that although his men will do as he says nine times out of ten, there may be occasions when a player who has seized the ball will see that it is better to do something else. In loose scrums and mauls, the leader's job is vital, for if there is no single mind directing operations, you might have five forwards trying to take, and three trying to heel! So when the leader calls " Take ", all eight forwards must take, and when he whips out " Now heel ", everyone must strive to get the ball out.

Yet another of the duties of the pack leader is to work out, in conjunction with the captain, a series of plans for replacing injured players. A good general rule is that a disabled outside must always be replaced; Scotland's attempt to play England in 1949 with three three-quarters, keeping the sound wing three-quarter always on the open side, was not successful. The scrum must be rearranged to pack 3–4, which is simply the 3–4–1 formation without the lock.

But to be their tactical chief is only half the pack-leader's job, for he should be the " heart " as well as the " head " of the forwards. With words of exhortation and encouragement—rarely of blame—and even sometimes with merely a bull-like roar, he must keep his eight going as hard as they can from the first whistle to the last. He must, in fact, keep alive in them the will to win.

CHAPTER VII

OUTSIDE PLAY

To be an outside player without any weaknesses, certain essentials, such as quick starting, swerving, catching, passing, and tackling, must be mastered. Some of these are more important for certain positions than for others; for instance, while a scrum-half is rarely called upon to field a ball by catching it, a full-back is often required to do so. Some of these skills have been dealt with in Chapter IV as " Basic Principles ", but two which are particularly applicable to outside players are running with the ball and passing on the run.

Running with the Ball

For a forward, running is just a method for getting from one part of the field to another as quickly as possible. Except for the wing-forwards, who often join with the outsides in attack, few forwards expect to run far with the ball in their possession. But for the outside, the reverse is the case; he will usually run with the ball as far as the opposition will allow him. It is clearly more suitable, then, for a fast runner to play outside the scrum rather than in it. To the outside player, Rugger is a game of short episodes, each of which is like a 30 or 40 yards' sprint.

At the same time, the player who would win a 50 yards' race is not necessarily going to appear the fastest three-quarter, and certainly he is not necessarily the most dangerous. In a race, you have an un-interrupted run for a given distance, but on the Rugger field the player has to thread his way through a number of openings, and he must create those openings by deceiving his opponents as to his intended direction.

There is no doubt that certain players possess a natural gift for effective running which no amount of instruction will impart to another player who has little natural talent. However, there are a number of hints which can be given in the hope that a young player may absorb some by practice. First, every-one can aim at " quickness off the mark ". This quickness involves good anticipation and then rapid acceleration, the former coming largely from experi-ence of the game. There are two secrets for quick starting—keep on your toes with heels off the ground, and start with small steps so that you gradually lengthen your stride to its best length. The advice that any trainer will give a sprinter can well be applied to the start of each episode for outside play, with a few obvious exceptions and alterations. For instance, the Rugger player cannot prepare a starting place, neither can he use his arms like a sprinter at such a time as he is receiving or holding the ball.

In actual play, an outside rarely has to run from a " standing start ". When, for example, the ball is about to come out of a scrum, the stand-off half and the three-quarters will start to move forwards, taking the first few strides at a walking pace; then, as the ball is actually on its way, each player will accelerate. The best practice for this quickness off the mark is therefore as follows:

1. Stand in a normal position.
2. Rise on to your toes and walk a few paces forward.
3. Start a sprint, with short paces that gradually lengthen.
4. Having run about 15 yards, drop back to a walking pace.
5. Repeat the 15-yard sprint, and so on.

For the actual running, the arms must be used to hold the ball, instead of being used in a counter-motion to the legs as in a racing sprint. You should practise running with the ball ready for a pass to be given at any required moment; if you are a wing three-quarter, though, you should tuck the ball under one arm and run with the other arm being used mainly as for a racing sprint but occasionally for a hand-off. It is at this stage that you can try to develop the technique of what may be called the naturally gifted three-quarter. Such players can be seen to thread their way past a whole number of would-be tacklers. The various separate techniques of such a player are: (a) The Swerve, (b) The Side-step, (c) Variation of Pace, and (d) Selling a Dummy. Selling the dummy, being a pretended pass that actually is not given, is best described under the section on Passing.

(a) *The Swerve.* The swerve is essentially a quick change in direction of the body from the knees upward, while the feet continue to move smoothly forward along a form of S-bend. The body is made to lean over away from the expected tackle, and the balance is maintained by a slight crossing over of the feet. As this is such an important device for any outside, the following analytical exercise is suggested. The ideal conditions for carrying it out are those which preserve your feet marks, such as a light covering of snow on the ground, or a firm, sandy beach, or an indoor floor that would show the tread of wet feet. Those conditions are far removed from the normal conditions on a Rugger field, but if there are two or more of you to practise, you can watch each other's placing of the feet and compare them with the following diagrams.

Fig. (i) shows an S-bend marked out on the ground. If you run normally along such a curved course, your feet will be placed on either side of the line as shown, and your body will be carried in a vertical position nearly all the time, although at the point A it may lean slightly to the left to help the motion round the bend. Fig. (ii) shows the same course taken, but with a swerve at A. Hence the body is thrown over to the right; this causes you to lose your balance momentarily, so that the left foot has to come across the front of the right for one pace, after which the normal running is resumed. It is a good tip to practise with a ball in the hands; run down the curved line, remembering to swing your arms across to the left at the same time as you throw your body across to the right. Aim to make the whole run smooth; it should not consist of a series of jerky

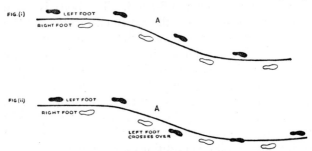

movements. Young boys with a natural gift for games will probably learn to swerve quite successfully by merely copying others who are adepts at it.

(b) *The Side-step*. The side-step is a relatively easy process to describe. When a player with the ball

is about to meet an opponent in the position of the post in Fig. (iii), instead of placing this right foot in the dotted position, he carries it across to the right by a kind of small hop. The body maintains a normal upright position in comparison with the swerve movement. There is little difficulty in carrying out this side-step at a slow pace; the main problem is to insert a side-step into a fast run without loss of forward pace. In the case of a side-step to the right, it requires a strong push by the *left* leg to carry the whole body to the right and then a strong *forward* push from the right foot to regain the forward pace. Light players with a strong stride are generally the best exponents of this useful form of evasive running.

(c) *Variation of Pace.* Every outside player should be told to run all out so long as he has the ball or is expecting to receive a pass. Outsides enjoy plenty of intervals of rest while scrums or line-outs are taking place, so when their turn does come, they must make the most of it. Some players fail to run all out because they know that the faster they are going the faster will they meet the ground when tackled! There is, therefore, a natural tendency to slow up when near an opponent; this should be avoided at all costs. Once this " all-out running " has been instilled into a player, variation of pace is a useful device, especially for the wing three-quarters. To a good tackler, an opponent who keeps to a steady course at a uniform pace is easy to bring down, because the tackler can estimate precisely his moment for " take-off ". Suppose, for example, that an attacking player A hopes to score a try just in the corner, while a defending player B is running along the dotted line so that a tackle seems inevitable. If A cannot run any faster, he can slow down his pace when he reaches the point X; B will then realise that he will overshoot his man. B must either slow up or change direction to the right, but as soon as A sees B's reaction to his ruse he can accelerate back to his former maximum speed. B may, of course, do the same, but he will probably not start soon enough to make his tackle and so prevent A from scoring his try. When three-quarters are practising a passing movement and have a clear run-in, they should therefore

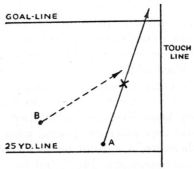

go all out, then check their pace for a few steps before going all out again. This checking is best done by a slight slackening of pace, but it can also be done by a temporary change to shorter paces.

Holding and Passing the Ball

(a) *Holding.* Every outside has to handle the ball, that is, to receive the ball, hold it for a time, and then pass it on to a colleague. Forwards also have occasional chances for inter-passing. Now unless the ball is held correctly, good passing is quite impossible. The correct hold is the natural one of having the fingers pointing down the length of the ball; the fingers should be opened apart and the thumbs curved well round the ball. When a ball is received from either a pass or a catch, it will not be gathered with this proper grip, so it should be the natural practice of every player to transfer the ball in his hands to the correct grip as quickly as possible.

(b) *Passing*. The correct passing movement, not only of arms but also of body and legs, is the most important of all essentials for an outside player, including wing forwards. The whole movement is a co-ordination of wrists, arms, hips, and legs. Like

RIGHT   **WRONG**

many other co-ordinated movements (as, for example, swimming), much patience and practice are required to perfect the passing technique.

First of all, practise the arm-and-body movement while almost stationary. Hold the ball correctly as already described and allow the arms to move freely across the body from right to left and back again. The arms should not be stiff, but should bend slightly in a natural way at the elbows; and the ball should travel in a straight line, not in a curve.

In order to achieve this, the arms must clearly move away from the body at the end of the swing. The next stage is to introduce some body movement. If the pass is to be to the left, move the right foot forward and turn the body to the left as the arms swing to the left. Allow the arms to swing out to their full extent and then let go of the ball so that it travels in a direction just above the horizontal. Practise with a partner receiving the ball; take two swings of the arms, then move the right leg forward, turn the body, and pass the ball to your partner about 3 yards away on the left. Because most people are right-handed, the pass to the left is generally easier than the one to the right; it is important, therefore, to practise both ways.

Let us now consider what part your head and eyes are going to play during a pass. As will be emphasised for receiving a pass, your eyes must be kept on the ball all the time. Once the ball is safely in your hands, the next reaction will be to look ahead to ascertain the position of your opponents. You must then quickly decide upon your intentions, whether to try a break-through or to draw a man and pass. Suppose the second choice is made and your partner is on your left; you then turn your head and body slightly to the left. It usually happens that when the ball is moving across a three-quarter line to the left, the direction of running for each player will also be slightly to the left of a line straight down the field. So just before he passes the ball, each player straightens out his run, as in the diagram on the next page.

This has the object of drawing your opposite number, but it also represents what should actually happen when a pass is given. During the run before giving the pass, the body and head will be turned to the left, with one eye on your partner and

one eye on your opposite number, if you can over-
come this optical problem! Then you straighten
your run, throw your weight on to the outside of
the right foot and carry the arms across to the
right. Next you rotate your body from the hips to
the left. This causes you to lean farther over to
the right, so your left foot as it comes forward must
cross over to prevent you falling. During this turn

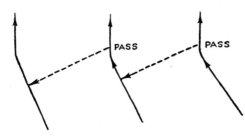

of the body and hips, the arms move straight away
from your body, which now faces your partner, so
that you have both eyes looking at him.

One important point remains—the use of the
wrists. The movement of the wrists can make the
final adjustment to the flight of the ball. When
your partner is really near, the ball can travel
horizontally between you; if, on the other hand,
he is some distance away, the ball will have to leave
your hands with a slightly upward trajectory. The
wrists have to control this trajectory of the ball,
and they can also influence slightly the direction of
flight, which is, of course, mainly decided by the
arm movement.

(c) *Receiving a Pass.* When a passing movement breaks down between two players, either the giver or the receiver of the pass may be to blame. If the receiver is to blame, the fault will almost certainly be due to not keeping both eyes on the ball until it is safely held, or not being prepared to receive the pass. When you are running alongside the player with the ball, you should try to watch both him and the opposition at the same time, but as soon as the pass is given, you should concentrate entirely on the ball; only when it is safely in your hands should you look up again at the opposition in order to decide on your plan of action. When the ball is dry, it can be caught like a cricket ball by both the hands closing round it. You should then immediately change to the correct grip, unless you have a clear run in front of you; in that case, the ball can be tucked along one arm, while the other arm is used for handing-off. As in cricket, do not snatch at the ball, but rather allow it to come smoothly into a cup made by the two hands. When the ball is slippery, it is difficult to make a clean catch. Whenever possible, however, get both hands and arms underneath the ball, and as it lands upon them bring the hands up so that it is held between the arms and the chest. It is a good tip to practise passing when the grass is wet, so that you can experiment with and without mittens to find out if you prefer them.

(d) *Running on to a Pass.* This phrase is used to describe the acceleration which everyone receiving a pass should try to make as the ball is just reaching him. The object is for the player, especially if he is a wing three-quarter, to be moving at his maximum speed when he has gone only a few yards with the ball. If you over-run a pass, it is obvious that you must slow up, but as this is most undesirable, your partner should try to pass the ball well in front of you; in that way, you can speed up from the moment that the ball leaves his hand. A long, slightly lobbed pass given well in front of a player gives him the best chance to accelerate and to run on to his pass, because he has just that extra fraction of time for running before making his catch.

Difficult Passes to Take. Whenever your partner gives you a bad pass, it is your job to make the best of it and not to stop playing in disgust, so the following hints may be useful. If the pass comes behind you, use one hand and turn your body more than usual towards the ball. You will probably have to slow up to help the difficulty of the one hand gathering the ball, but, if at all possible, avoid that. If the ball comes too low, perhaps below the level of your knees, there is nothing for it but to bend well down and use *both* hands. Some players, especially younger ones, can continue running almost at full speed with their hands nearly touching the ground. If the ball comes too high, but at the right position in front of you, there should not be any special difficulty in gathering it; the chief problem is to avoid a knock-on. An important point to remember is that when you cannot gather a pass with your hands, you can *use your feet*. Many a promising attack can be carried on by foot work, whereas a knock-on resulting from trying to gather a low pass will stop the movement altogether. Wing three-quarters should definitely practise utilising a ball passed too much in front of them by kicking parallel to the touch-line to such a position that they can be the first to reach the ball and then continue the foot-work. On a wet day, when passes are more likely to go astray, flying kicks down the field often gain much ground, especially if they are judiciously placed relative to the position of the opposing full-back.

TACTICS FOR THE VARIOUS OUTSIDE POSITIONS

Two qualities make up the good player, the physical—athletic ability, physique, and technique—and the mental—knowledge of the game, experience, and a natural gift for tactics. The young player who has just left school has most of the physical qualities, but probably lacks the mental ones. The player over thirty-five, on the other hand, will have lost his physical but gained in mental requirements. Selectors are thus often forced to choose between a young and an old player, each of whom may be of about equal value to their side. By the time a player is between twenty-five and thirty, he should be combining many of the " ideal requirements " and therefore be in his prime.

I. SCRUM-HALF

The essential requirement from a scrum-half is an ability to get the ball away quickly and accurately to those behind him. For this he requires quick co-ordination of hands and feet. He need not have the weight of a forward or the speed in running of a three-quarter, but he must have considerable strength in body and arms to give a long pass off the ground and to get through much defensive work against the opposing forwards.

In school football, the general tendency is to group the heavy boys as forwards and the faster runners as three-quarters; the remainder—the light or slow ones—tend to begin as scrum-halves or full-backs, irrespective of their other qualities. This is a general mistake. The scrum-half is the most important player on the field, because nearly every attacking movement starts from him, and the best player for that position should be chosen *first* and not last. It is true that the typical scrum-half is a short, stocky, nippy player, but there have been many great internationals, especially from overseas, who have been quite 6 feet tall and of such a build that they might well have played in the pack. However, the vital quality for the position is quick co-ordination of feet and arms, combined with a natural instinct to start the right movement for the occasion; and such qualities may be possessed by a player who is 5 or 6 feet tall and 9 or 13 stones in weight.

Passing Off the Ground. A player has the choice of two methods—the falling and the non-falling. The first method is better for boys under sixteen, because it produces a longer and more accurate pass by anyone who has not grown to full strength; the second method is used, with a few variations, by most mature players.

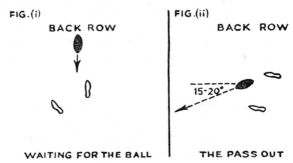

Learning the Falling Method.

STAGE I.   Passing to the Left.

Take up your stance as if waiting for the ball. The body faces half-left—the expected direction of the pass—with the right foot pointing forward and the left foot farther back and to the left, as in Fig. (i). Bend the knees and adopt a sitting position with the fingers touching the ground. If possible, get someone to roll the ball back towards you as it would come from a perfect heel from the back row of the scrum. As the ball comes towards your left foot, move the right as shown in Fig. (ii).

This carries your body round so that you are almost facing your partner, or rather the place where your partner should be when taking the pass. This direction of pass is usually about 20° back. This footwork is most important, and is worth practising on its own, first to balls which come out of the scrum in an ideal manner, and then to those which come out suddenly at the sides. In the latter, the footwork has to be adjusted rapidly to the corresponding positions, and agility is obviously essential for a scrum-half.

STAGE 2. Making the Pass.

Hold the ball firmly, with the hands rather underneath the ball, keep the knees well bent as you lean to the left, and let your arms move away from you as you face the direction in which the ball is to travel. This will bring your weight on to your toes, and as your arms continue to move, you will lose your balance. At this point you straighten your legs, thus making the upper part of your body accelerate. The ball is now released, and the arms follow through for the moment in the required direction. By this time your face is about to meet the ground, but your arms are quickly brought down to break your fall. The criticism of this falling method is that the scrum-half is now on the ground out of action; but this need not be the case if he will spring quickly to his feet again. The real danger is that it is difficult to change your plan once you have begun to lose your balance; all the same, small boys certainly can give good, reliable long passes in this way.

Learning the Non-Falling Method.

STAGE 1.   Passing to the Left.

The scrum-half waits for the ball with both feet pointing forward.   If it is intended to pass to the left, the left foot will be slightly back, but the player can easily alter his intentions at the last moment.   From Fig. (i) to Fig. (ii), the ball has appeared from the back row of the forwards, and the right foot has moved slightly forward while the left foot has pivoted round;   the player is still almost facing to the front.   The hands grasp the ball while the knees are bent, though not so much as in the falling method.

STAGE 2.   Making the Pass.

The method is similar to that of passing on the run, except, of course, that the feet are almost stationary.   As the arms move across to the left, the hips revolve and give force to the arm movement.   All the weight is taken on the right foot, so that the left foot can move away and then take the weight as it is transferred sideways.   As the whole movement is a vigorous one, the right foot will have to move beyond the left, and this will start the player on the move.   The main advantage of this method is that the player can alter his intentions; if he

spots an opponent advancing for the interception, he can withhold the pass and start a
run.

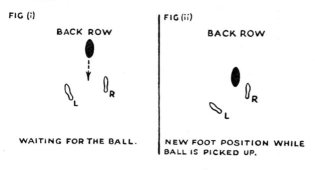

FIG (i)

BACK ROW

WAITING FOR THE BALL.

FIG (ii)

BACK ROW

NEW FOOT POSITION WHILE
BALL IS PICKED UP.

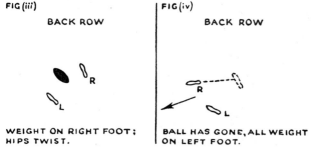

FIG (iii)

BACK ROW

WEIGHT ON RIGHT FOOT;
HIPS TWIST.

FIG (iv)

BACK ROW

BALL HAS GONE, ALL WEIGHT
ON LEFT FOOT.

**Important Points Common to both Methods of Passing from
the Scrum**

(1) Play as close as you can to the fixed and
loose scrums; even a yard away is often too far.

(2) In whatever way the ball rolls towards you,
try to grip it correctly.

(3) As you make the pass, the ball should fly with its long axis pointing to your partner.

(4) The pass must be off the ground; do not first pick up the ball and *then* make the pass, as this merely wastes a vital tenth of a second.

Passing Practice through a Hoop

Obtain a child's hoop about 3 feet in diameter, and hang it from the cross-bar between two high-jump standards, so that the bottom of the hoop is about 18 inches off the ground. Then place a post along the 25-yard- or half-way line of the field, as in the diagram (plan):

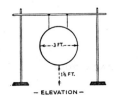 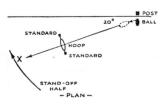

Mark out with a white line the 20° angle back from the line selected (some stand-off halves or coaches may prefer a larger angle). At a convenient distance, depending upon the age and strength of the scrum-half, place the upright standards and the hanging hoop. The object is for the scrum-half to pass the ball through the middle of the hoop and for the stand-off half to take it on the run at the point X. The advantage of this form of combined practice is that when a pass is not gathered, the player at fault can be checked up at once; for instance, so long as the ball goes through the hoop at a reasonable pace, the scrum-half cannot be blamed. Remember that, since just as many passes have to be sent out to the right as to the left, the hoop must be changed across to the other side at intervals.

The Reverse Pass

Let us imagine that the scrum-half has his partner and the majority of the three-quarter line arranged

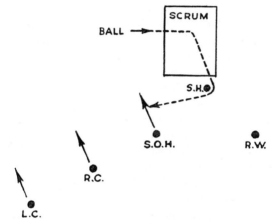

on the left of the field, as in the above diagram. The ball is heeled, but instead of coming through the middle of the back row, it comes out on the right-hand side. The scrum-half then has two choices: either to make a normal pass to his right-wing three-quarter or to make a " reverse pass " to his stand-off half. The latter is generally the better, and is a useful move which often deceives the

opposition. The scrum-half begins as if he is going
to pass to the right, but while his knees are still
bent he swings right round by pivoting on his right
foot with the ball held out in front of him. During
the first part of the swing he will not be able to
see his partner, but as he turns farther round, the
stand-off half will come into view and the ball is
propelled away just in front of him.

The various parts played by a scrum-half can
best be illustrated by describing five incidents in an
imaginary game. The diagram (on p. 159) shows the
five positions from which each episode of play
starts. At Position (1) a scrum is given because
of a knock-on by the Blacks. If you are the White
scrum-half, it is your job to put the ball into the
scrum from the left side as you face up the field,
because your scrum has the loose head there. You
must stand 3 feet from the side of the scrum, hold
the ball normally just above the ground, and as
soon as the scrum is steady, you swing your arms
so that the ball lands full pitch beyond the feet of
the outside men of the scrum's front row. Just
before you put the ball in, you give your side
warning with some such phrase as " Coming in left,
Whites. . . . Now! " Assuming that your hooker
succeeds in obtaining possession, you quickly whip
round to the back of your scrum. As the scrum is
near your goal-line, and remembering that useful
slogan " Never pass in your own twenty-five ", you
make a quick punt into touch before an opposing
forward smothers you. Clearing the heads of the

THE VARIOUS TACTICS FOR A SCRUM-HALF

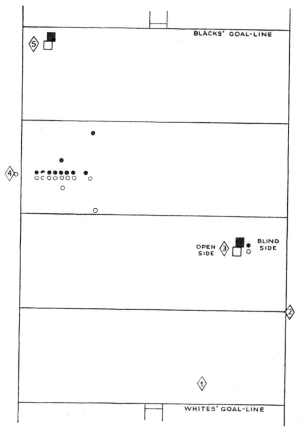

players in front of you, you manage to find touch near the 25-yard line.

That brings us to Position (2). Here Blacks

F

throw the ball in, and your job is to help your scrum leader by spotting any opposing forward who is unmarked in the line-out; you can also reinforce any instructions he gives. As you are still on the defensive, the orders will probably be " Put the ball down and take ". Your forwards manage to do this, but an accidental off-side stops their dribble, and a scrum is ordered at Position (3).

It is now the job of your opposite number to put the ball in, and you must always mark him by standing alongside. You will therefore both start on the " blind side " of the scrum, and as the Blacks obtain the ball, your role is a defensive one. You must be careful to keep *both* your feet behind the ball as Blacks try to heel, but you mark the opposing scrum-half as closely as the laws allow, ready to smother him as soon as the ball comes out. It is particularly important that you do not allow him to run round you on the blind side. After some loose play by the Black outsides, the ball goes into touch at Position (4).

Note your position at the line-out as shown in the diagram; a forward should pass the ball back to you only if he can do it *immediately*; any hesitation is fatal. As the ball is thrown in, and whilst it is in the air, you must move so as to be behind the man who is likely to catch it. We will imagine the throw is followed by a loose scrum; Whites heel the ball rather on the left side, so now is your chance for a blind-side movement with your wing three-quarter. Do not just pass the ball to him and expect him to make his way along the blind side, where he will meet his opposite number, but rather set off on your own to draw that wing three-quarter. Your own blind-side wing forward should also be up to join in this movement, which, with a weak opposition, often gains much ground.

The next imaginary incident to complete our game is at Position (5), where a fixed scrum is ordered only a few yards from Blacks' goal-line. If Whites obtain possession of the ball, the scrum-half has a difficult choice between a normal pass out to his stand-off half or a sharp dash for the line on his own. The choice, of course, depends on the circumstances of the moment. If the opposing wing forwards go for the interception, you should hold your pass, dart forward, and literally dive the last few yards for the line. It is in such circumstances that a heavy scrum-half will score a try when a lighter player may not; in any case, it is very difficult for a defence to stop a determined scrum-half when he receives the ball from a scrum close to his opponents' goal-line.

The reader will note that during all these five episodes, Whites' scrum-half has not given a single pass to his stand-off. These examples have been chosen purposely to illustrate the various choices that should be in a scrum-half's mind *apart* from the normal one of passing. It must, therefore, be strongly re-emphasised that the prime duty of a scrum-half is to feed his outsides with a stream of accurate passes; his quality stands or falls by that.

At the same time, it is the unexpected which so often succeeds; so when he has given a dozen passes one way and the other to his outsides, he can suddenly make a run on his own with considerable probability of success. Yet that final dash for a try should be made only if success is almost certain.

Giving Instructions

There are only three players who should use their voices during a game; they are the captain, the leader of the forwards, and the scrum-half. The scrum-half's contribution will vary according to his experience. The minimum essential is that he must tell his forwards when and where to break—" Break right," or " Break—Blind Side ". To this essential can be added a form of useful running commentary during all scrums, especially loose ones, because he is in the best position for seeing what is happening to the ball. In fact, he is often in a better position than the scrum leader to see when a dribble should be carried on or when a loose scrum should form for a quick heel. Whatever he says should be encouraging to the forwards; it is the duty of the captain or the scrum leader to point out their deficiencies. Finally, in addition to all the above-mentioned jobs and responsibilities, the scrum-half has one further duty to perform in defence—he must fall on the ball at the earliest opportunity whenever his opponents start a dribble.

2. STAND-OFF HALF

The vital requisite of a stand-off half is that he should be able to take a pass thrown out by his scrum-half and then to give such a pass to one of his centres that the latter is at that moment travelling at full speed. Consequently, the outside half, as he is sometimes called, must from a standing start take the ball while on the run and accelerate as much as possible.

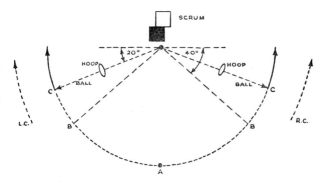

The position of the stand-off half behind the fixed or loose scrum is a matter of importance. There is no definite rule; every player must work out with his partner the best angles for the pass and his own starting point. The above diagram illustrates various cases. The ideal is for the stand-off half to take up his position at A directly behind the scrum; then when he sees his partner is about to obtain possession he can shout " Left " or

" Right ".   If he is very quick off the mark and if the scrum-half throws a long pass, he ought to be able to reach C by the time the ball reaches him. This ideal has the great advantage that the halves can develop the attack on either side of the scrum, but only at international standards can such a plan be carried out successfully.   The stand-off, therefore, usually takes up his position somewhere along the curved line between A and C.   The position B, at 40°, is about the average, although much depends on the conditions.   On a dry calm day at the beginning of the game, the stand-off half may be 10 yards away and 50° back; on a wet day towards the end of the game he may be only 5 yards away and 25° back.

The direction of run is also important.   The stand-off half must get away from opposition forwards, and for that reason he should run at about 45° from the line straight down the field for a few paces.   As he is about to pass, he should straighten up, that is, run deliberately towards his opponents. In order to practise, the hoop can be set up as previously suggested, the scrum-half throws out his pass, the stand-off takes the ball as it comes across his body in front of him, and, when he has taken four or five paces, passes it on to his centre.   Do not run *towards* the ball as the scrum-half passes, or that will take you too near the scrum.   Such practices between halves and centres will prove invaluable in match play.

Alternative Methods of Attack.

Just as the success of a scrum-half depends upon his passes out from the scrum, so that of the stand-off depends on the passes he gives to his centres. The aim of the stand-off is to get his line of three-quarters moving at top speed. However, his passes must not be so mechanical that his opponents know he will *always* pass; in that case, they can concentrate on tackling and subduing the centres. The opponents must be kept guessing, and whenever possible must be taken by surprise. It is the stand-off half who is in the best position to vary the tactics. For every four orthodox passes given to a three-quarter, one of the following variations should be tried:

(*a*) Swerve past your opposite stand-off half.

(*b*) Kick high up the middle of the field and follow up rapidly.

(*c*) Kick diagonally towards touch, taking care to avoid the opposing full back.

(*d*) Pass back to the scrum-half or a wing forward.

(*e*) Make a defensive kick to touch.

(*f*) Drop-kick when in front of goal.

The first of these, the swerve or cut-in, requires some analysing. The stand-off half must always remember that he has more than his opposite number marking him. Reference to the chapter on Forward Play in defence will show that at least the open-side wing forward will be detailed to go

for him.   Diagram [A] shows the common temptation
for a stand-off to cut-in between his opposite number
and the scrum. When he first receives the ball,
there appears to be a tempting space, but as he
moves into it he will find that it will soon be covered
by the opposing back-row forwards.   In the following three diagrams, A, B, and C, the positions of

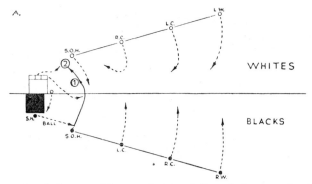

each of the outsides, and especially of the stand-off
half, should be carefully studied.

On the line representing the course of the Black
stand-off half, there are two arrows (1) and (2).
The first arrow shows his approximate position at
the same time as all the other players have reached
their " arrow positions ".   The second arrow shows
his position after another short interval.   If we
imagine all the other players to have run a corresponding distance, the resulting confusion can well
be judged.   The two White back-row forwards and
the right centre will all have converged and shut in

the Black stand-off half, so that he will have little chance of passing to an unmarked colleague.

Diagram [A], then, represents the cut-in swerve which comes to nothing.

Diagram [B] shows how the cut-in swerve may be successful against *slow* defence. Note that all the Black moves are the same, except that the scrum-half, seeing his partner cut-in, has this time made a special effort and gone farther. Whites,

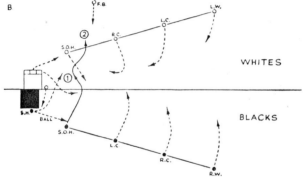

however, have reacted slowly; the wing forward has not gone across sufficiently, and the right centre has not turned back soon enough. Note that the Black stand-off half, after cutting in, has swerved out again away from the scrum, and now stands a good chance of evading the " lock " of Whites' scrum; but note also that he has cut himself off from his own three-quarters. He will soon be meeting the White full-back, when he may be able to pass to his scrum-half or a wing forward who

G

may have managed to back up; otherwise he will
have to continue with a solo effort.

Diagram [B], then, illustrates a cut-in and swerve-
out which will be successful only against slow defence
or as the result of a very quick heel. It is always
worth trying at least twice in a game, but no more
unless it is successful.

Diagram [C] shows how the Black stand-off half
can draw not only his opposite number but also a

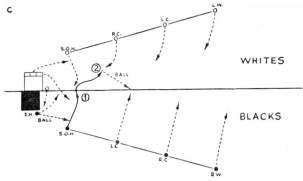

centre, and then pass. He thus creates a man over
for his three-quarters. This is done by feinting to
cut-in; this causes the White right centre to alter
his course, as in the previous diagrams. The half
then swerves out, so that he has both his opposite
number and the right centre coming to tackle him.
He can then pass to his own left centre, and if his
three-quarters make no mistake, the wing should
have a clear run until he meets the White full-
back. The stand-off half must not try to draw the

opposite centres by running across in an effort to outflank them. If he does this, he will only crowd his three-quarters together and give them no chance. In fact, as soon as any player finds himself running across the field, he should change direction forward and then pass or kick.

Final Hints for the Stand-off Half

(1) Be quick off the mark and take your pass at full speed.

(2) Get your passes out to your three-quarters quickly, especially at the start of the game.

(3) Vary your tactics as the game progresses.

(4) Do not run across the field.

3. CENTRE THREE-QUARTER

From a physical point of view, centre three-quarters should be strongly built yet able to run fast, with an ability to swerve or side-step. They must also be able to pass well, to time their passes correctly, to tackle (often in head-on tackles), and to kick well, although this last asset is not so essential as the other skills. The play of centre three-quarters is very similar to that of the stand-off half, and many good players have changed from one of these positions to the other. Whereas the stand-off can often start to make openings for the centres, the centres have to carry on and either break through the defence themselves or else create a clear run for their partner on the wing. The centre should therefore be a heavier player, so that his momentum will carry him through small gaps. He must also acquire " an eye for an opening ". As soon as he is about to receive a pass, he should be able to size-up the positions of his opponents and decide whether he can squeeze through a gap or whether he should draw his man and pass. To pass when he should have found a gap is wrong; to be tackled in possession when he tried to go through and failed is equally wrong. This eye for an opening cannot be taught or practised; it is a matter of experience and natural gifts. A coach will, of course, tell a centre when he has made the wrong move, but that does not guarantee he will make the correct choice next time.

There are numerous combined movements which the whole three-quarter line can exploit. If you have taught yourself the essentials of running, passing, and tackling, and if you possess the physique to be chosen as a centre, you will no doubt practise with the other outsides in these various combined movements and, if fortunate, be coached at the same time.

Position Play.

In association football and hockey, each player has a more or less correct position on the field which he maintains relative to the position of the ball. In Rugby football, all the forwards and the scrum-half do their best to be " on the ball " wherever it is in the field; they do not stand waiting for the ball to come to them. The remaining players—stand-

off half, three-quarters, and full-back—have to keep
correct positions relative to each other and to the
position of the ball. The stand-off's position is
fairly easy, but the centres have a more difficult
task, and most players playing there for the first
time are rather lost. The general principle is that
they " line back " from either the stand-off half or
the scrum.

In the two diagrams below, the first shows a
fixed scrum slightly to the left of mid-field. For
such a position, one centre—the left—will be on one

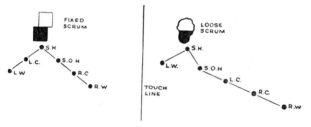

side of the scrum prepared to receive a pass from
the scrum-half, while the right centre will line back
from his stand-off half. The second diagram illustrates what happens if a loose scrum forms nearer
the touch-line. In this case the left centre has to
line back on the stand-off half with the other three-
quarters beyond and outside him. Sometimes it is
an advantage to have the same player as an " inside " centre always next to the stand-off, with the
other centre always beyond him, but that is a matter
of major tactics. It is important that the centres
should return to their standard positions as soon as

possible after being tackled or involved amongst
the forwards. It is more important still that the
threes advance as a line, whether in attack or
defence. If one player moves up to his opponents
quickly and another slowly, the line will become
zig-zag and cease to be straight. This is exactly
what the opposition want, because there will then
be a gap which cannot be covered even by the best
tackling. Study this diagram:

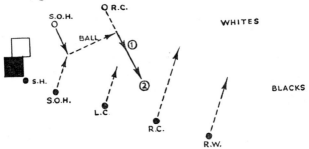

The Black right-centre has advanced out of line,
so when the White right-centre receives the ball and
has gone a few paces he will be at the position of
his arrow (1), while all others will be at their
arrow-heads. There is nothing then to stop the
White right-centre from moving on to his second
position (2). If the Black right-centre had kept
back in line with his other three-quarters, no such
gap would have appeared.

Selling a Dummy.

This phrase—selling a dummy—has long been
used for a feint which the player with the ball can

make so that a would-be tackler believes he is going to pass the ball and therefore fails to make his tackle. The would-be tackler is said to " buy the dummy ". When a centre has gone through an opening, he usually finds himself cut off and unable to pass safely to a colleague. However, by going through the motions of passing, he can often deceive the opponent who should tackle him.

The art of selling the dummy lies in correct or even exaggerated arm and hip work, as described in the section on " Passing ". If a feint to pass to the left is to be made, the arms should be taken well across to the right as the left foot comes forward. During the next pace with the right foot, the hips are revolved and the arms move across as if to pass, but the ball, which must be firmly held, is not allowed to leave the hands, which are brought back at the last possible moment. By this time, the player should be leaning well over to his right, and he will have to bring his left foot across to prevent himself from falling over. This partial fall to the right, however, will take the player away from his opponent, who, he hopes, will buy the dummy by going after the expected flight of the ball. When properly executed, this movement can be one of the most attractive in the game, and some gifted players can make their way through a bewildered defence selling dummies to right and left.

Other Tactics for Centres are :

(1) The short punt ahead over the opposing

three-quarters, but short of the full-back. This is specially useful when the opposition is lying well up for defence.

(2) The diagonal kick towards the touch-line. The object here is for the wing three-quarter to reach and gather the ball before the opposing full-back. This kick is usually a sign of weakness, suggesting that the three-quarter line cannot do anything by passing; even so, it is better than passing to a partner who is obviously well marked.

(3) A return or reverse pass to a half or a wing forward. This often catches the defence on the wrong foot. The centre shapes as if to pass normally to his other centre or wing, but turns round the reverse way to pass inwards instead of outwards. The main difficulty is for the centre to know exactly where his colleague is, and only combined practice will enable such manœuvres to come off during match play.

Final Hints for Centres

(1) Run as fast as possible and draw your opposite number before passing.

(2) Exploit all gaps offered by the opposing defence.

(3) Always advance in line, and always tackle the man with the ball.

(4) Do not run across the field.

(5) Do not pass to a partner who is already well marked; it is better to " die with the ball ".

So much, then, for centre three-quarter play.

Let us now turn to:

4. WING THREE-QUARTER

The essential qualities for a wing three-quarter are fast and determined running, with an ability to side-step or swerve, and good tackling. No special kicking ability is required, but control of the ball as in soccer is often valuable. The wing

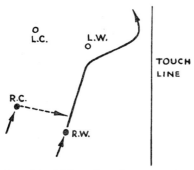

three-quarter should be the player to finish off the attacks initiated by the other outsides. He should always try to keep a few yards away from his inside partner and a yard or two behind him, no matter where the inside goes. Consequently, if his inside cuts through the centre, the wing must also squeeze through after him in order to keep alongside; if the inside has to run across the field, the wing must also run across, in order to keep away from him. In other words, he must always position himself for the final pass. As that pass comes towards him, he should accelerate to his top speed and aim to run *outside* his opposite wing. Many tries are lost by wings who try to dodge inside an opponent instead of running out between him and the touch-line; a skilful player can often make his way for a long distance between the touch and 5-yard lines, even though he has little room in which to manœuvre. Similarly, when within sight of the

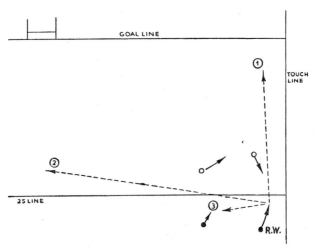

opponents' goal-line, a wing should always run towards the corner-flag, for in that way he has the best chance of avoiding defenders covering across. When you are clear of your opponents—and only then—you should attempt to score your try as near to the goal-posts as possible. Remember, too, that you should always carry the ball on the touch-line side of you, so as to be ready to hand-off on the inside.

The next important point for a wing to bear in mind is that he must at all costs keep up the attack. Therefore, unless you are in your own twenty-five, never kick the ball away into touch, even though you are expecting to be tackled. By putting the ball in touch, you see, you are giving your opponents a valuable chance to reorganise their defence.

The diagram on p. 178 shows a Black right wing about to be hemmed in by two defending White players. There are three possible ways of keeping the attack going. (1) A kick ahead parallel to the touch-line, in such a way that the wing will have a good chance of getting to the ball and dribbling it over the goal-line. (2) A cross kick high into the centre of the field, where any other Blacks who are on-side may gather a lucky bounce and sprint over for a try. (3) A pass inside to a colleague who is backing up. If you have only one opponent such as the full-back to beat, there should always be a good chance of avoiding his tackle. The methods for getting past such an opponent have already been described in the early part of this chapter.

It often happens, especially on a wet day, that the ball goes loose near the touch-line. This provides an opportunity for the wing to use his feet in much the same way as an outside right or left dribbles down the touch-line at soccer. There is no need, fortunately, to employ a controlled dribble; the ball can be kicked several yards ahead, without it going into touch, so that you have a good chance of getting a foot to it again before an opponent.

Then the ball is again kicked several yards, not necessarily straight ahead, but rather into an area where there is no opponent approaching. Finally, it can be kicked over the goal-line and touched down.

In defence, a wing three-quarter must mark his opposite wing. If you realise that he is a faster runner than you are, you must mark him very closely. So when the opposing outsides are hand-

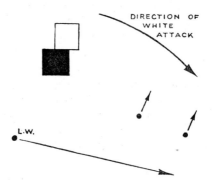

ling the ball, run up quickly to within a few yards of your opponent; then, just as he is receiving his pass, you should be within tackling range of him. A wing should always " cover back " when his opponents' attack is going the other way. In the diagram, Whites are attacking, as shown. In too many cases, the Black left wing stands still watching the result, probably a try against him! Yet if he runs back into the middle of the field towards his own goal, he will probably be able to help the defence and provide just that extra tackle required to prevent a try being scored. To summarise, then, wing three-quarters should run fast and towards—or parallel to—the touch-line; they should do their utmost to keep the attack going; as a general rule they should avoid kicking into touch; and they should mark their opposite wing closely.

5. FULL-BACK

The essential requirements for a full-back are that he should be a safe fielder of the ball, an accurate kicker—preferably with either foot—and a really reliable tackler. If he also possesses the ability to stop forward rushes by falling on the ball or whipping it off their feet, so much the better. If a captain has to choose for a full-back between a player who is quite safe at fielding and kicking, and one who is a good tackler, the former should be selected. It is most discouraging for forwards to have to go back 20 or 30 yards every time their full-back fumbles an opponent's kick.

A full-back definitely requires the right temperament. He wants a cool head and a sense of satisfaction in breaking down his opponents' attacks, rather than an ambition to attack himself. Yet an enterprising full-back can join in an attack by coming up on the end of his three-quarter line, with an occasional chance of scoring a try in that way. If you are selected to play full-back, you should, of course, practise to improve your kicking and fielding with some partner; and while you are doing this, you should aim to find touch as far down field as possible. In an actual game, you must not take the risk of failing to find touch; it is better to be sure of gaining 10 yards of ground than to fail by a few feet to gain 40 yards.

The Angle of Kick.

If an opponent kicks from mid-field and fails to find touch so that you, as full-back, catch the ball at position A in the following diagram, you should run out away from the touch-line into the field to the point B and then kick for touch yourself. In this way, you have a better chance of finding a long touch than if you kicked almost parallel to the

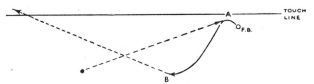

touch-line from near A. As soon as you realise that any kick is not going into touch, you must run forward as fast as you can in order to get in front of the remainder of your colleagues, thereby putting them on-side again. While you are doing this, the nearest three-quarter should drop back to take your place.

Position Play.

Once you have decided on full-back as your position, you should study carefully where you are going to place yourself at various times during a

game. You can best do this by watching the
movements of a first-class full-back; keep your eyes
on him and not on the ball, and you will soon
learn a good deal about the art of position play.
You will notice that he runs backwards and forwards across the field, probably without touching
the ball for long spells. Whenever his opponents
kick ahead, however, he will be ready to catch the
ball full pitch. This position play is largely a
matter of experience, but the following principles
are given as a general guide.

First of all, it is best to stand some 10 to 15 yards
behind your three-quarter line and opposite the
ball as the play moves from side to side. If you
are playing against a wind, this distance may have
to be increased to 30 yards, because you should
never allow your opponents to kick the ball over
your head, unless the ball will inevitably go over
the goal-line, where it can be touched down. By
standing only 10 yards behind the threes, you
have the best chance of tackling any opponent
who may have cut through the middle; once a
player is clear and has ample room in which to
manœuvre, he ought to be able to beat the full-
back fairly easily.

In order to be in the right place to field the ball,
it is necessary to watch your opponents very carefully. As soon as, say, the stand-off half has the
ball, he will start to run in one direction, and you
must duly follow him across. If you watch the
hands and arms of the player with the ball, you

can spot when he is about to pass and when to kick; as soon as you see him shaping to punt, you must anticipate the direction and start off almost before the ball has left his foot. Do not start *too* soon, on the other hand, or he will change direction at the last moment and catch you on the wrong foot. Much of the fascination of full-back play is the study of your opponents' tactics and the answers which you are going to make to them.

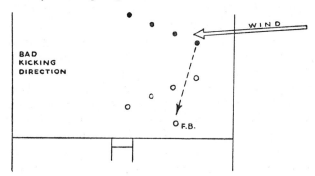

Playing in a Wind.

Suppose there is a cross wind as shown in this diagram, and a kick ahead is fielded by the White full-back; he has two difficult alternatives. One is to kick against the wind to the nearer touch-line, and the other is to kick right across to the far touch-line with help from the wind. If the rest of his side are in the right-hand side of the field, it is very risky to kick the ball away from them, because if the ball fails to find touch, the opposing wing three-quarter may pick it up and run in for a try. The back should therefore run as far as he can towards the right touch-line, and then kick with a low trajectory into the wind. It is bad play to make your forwards run across the field merely for a throw-in which could have been near them. When you are playing *with* the wind, kick as high as you can. As an exception to the general rule, a full-back can occasionally kick high down the field without the ball going into touch, provided he immediately follows up his kick.

The Aggressive Full-back.

Although a full-back is primarily a defensive player, he can occasionally adopt an offensive role. It has already been suggested that he can run up quickly and tack on to the end of the three-quarter line. Similarly, whenever he is in his opponents' half of the field and is able to gather a kick some distance from the touch-line, he can run forward and start a movement with his own three-quarters. This is generally known as " opening up the game ". A favourite trick of some full-backs is to take a few steps in one direction with the pretence of kicking for touch and then to start a movement by running in the opposite direction. A full-back sometimes has an opportunity to take a long drop-kick at goal; this occurs whenever his opponents are foolish enough to let him have the ball in their half of the field. A badly placed drop-out from a " twenty-five " will often provide such an opportunity.

To sum up, then, full-backs should practise kicking with each foot in turn, should always be certain of making touch when that is their intention, should never fail to follow up any bad or high kicks, and should always watch carefully the intentions of their opponents.   On the other hand, they should not kick away from their own colleagues, nor should they forget that they can with advantage start an attack to be carried on by their own three-quarters.

CHAPTER VIII

THE CONTROL OF THE GAME

THE game of Rugby football is controlled by a referee, with the help of two touch judges. As the reserve for a particular fifteen is often chosen automatically as touch judge, it is quite usual for any player to carry out that duty; refereeing, on the other hand, may be regarded as a more specialised job.

A Touch Judge is instructed to hold up his flag whenever the ball or a player carrying the ball goes into touch, and he must keep the flag up until the referee has stopped the game for a throw-in. He should realise that the white touch-line, and all the air vertically above it, is out of the field of play. If, therefore, a ball is blown back into the field after going over the line, touch should be signalled where the ball first crossed the vertical plane above the line. If a player holding the ball puts his foot on or over the line, he has gone out of play; yet a player dribbling the ball may run outside the line so long as the ball itself remains in play. The touch judge should indicate, by holding out one arm in the necessary direction, which side is entitled to the throw. When a player is really forced into touch, his team has the throw; when there is a doubt, the defending team should have the ball. The flag should be held up until the ball is fairly thrown in. If the wrong team throws in, or if there is any other irregularity, the flag should be kept up and not lowered.

When a player kicks the ball into touch near the corner-flag, it is most important to see which side of the flag it passed, that is, whether it was in touch or in touch-in-goal. Similarly, if a player with the ball is about to score near the corner-flag when he is tackled, he may just manage to ground the ball before hitting the post with his legs or he may hit it as he is falling to score; in such cases, the decision as to whether a try has been scored or not rests with the touch judge. Again, when the ball is kicked-off or dropped-out, it must not go full pitch into touch, and information on this point must be given to the referee.

The two touch judges also act as goal judges. After a try or a penalty-kick, when a player kicks for goal, each touch judge should place himself directly behind *one* post in line with the ball to be kicked. If the ball passes over the cross bar and inside the post under his immediate observation, he waves his flag; when the referee sees both flags waved, he signifies a goal.

For any reader of this book who really and sincerely wishes to teach himself the game of Rugger, the task of acting as a touch judge can be strongly recommended. The few rules enumerated above are all that are needed to enable any man or boy to enjoy taking part in a game, and while such a person will probably begin by showing an interest only, he will very soon teach himself all the fundamental principles of Rugger. Playing the game is obviously the best method, but if you are temporarily injured or not quite capable of making the grade in your club fifteen, touch judging is easily the next best thing, and can provide lots of fun to anyone who is really keen.

Refereeing

The essential duties of a referee are impartially to enforce the necessary laws, with the corresponding penalties, and at the same time to provide an enjoyable game for both sides. While being impartial, a referee should adjust his standard of strictness to the standard of game which he is controlling; this may vary from an international to a match between boys of twelve years of age. The general tendency, unfortunately, is for a game to have too many interruptions by the referee's whistle. While the referee should not allow any clear infringement of a law, he should allow the game to proceed with as few stoppages as possible. His chief opportunity comes from the use of the " advantage rule ". If one side errs by knocking-on or passing forward, the play should be allowed to continue to see what results; if the other side gain an advantage, they should be given the opportunity to develop it.

With regard to the knock-on, the referee has to set a standard in his own mind early in the game, though a recent amendment of the laws now gives him more discretion. Frequently a player taking a pass can let the ball rebound from his hands and yet catch it without allowing it to fall to the ground. In an international match any such visible rebound should be stopped and a scrum ordered; but in a boys' match, reasonable allowance may be permitted. It is important, however, for the referee to be consistent not only for both teams, but also throughout the game.

The off-side law should be enforced at all standards of Rugger, because off-side players, when they interfere, definitely spoil the game; and if they are not penalised, they will never learn that they are wrong. This leads to another important point—a referee should always make clear what infringement has caused him to blow his whistle. From this point of view, the model was T. H. Vile. In an international match he would stop the game, waggle his finger at some erring player, and give him a brief discourse on his mistake, just like a schoolmaster lecturing a small boy! Nevertheless, that player and most of the crowd knew exactly why the whistle had gone.

Rugger is a game in which high spirits and misplaced enthusiasm may get the upper hand of either a few players or a whole side, and it is the referee's duty to control the game in every sense of the word. Any game is liable to become discreditable if the laws are not applied properly in the early stages. If one side is allowed to gain an unfair advantage by illegal play, the referee is simply asking for trouble. Any sign, therefore, of

unfair practices during the first fifteen minutes
should be immediately pulled up and penalty-kicks
given against the offenders.   In fact, for the average
club match, all laws should be applied strictly during the first part of the game; then, when all the
players realise that the referee is really in control
and firm in his decisions, the game can be allowed
to continue with fewer stoppages for minor infringements.

For those who know the laws of the game but
have had little experience of actual refereeing, a
diagram showing the best positions for a referee,
where he can best see all that is happening without
getting in the way, is shown on p. 190.

This diagram shows at one and the same time
the suggested positions for a referee at a fixed scrum,
at a drop-out, at a line-out, and at a loose scrum
near the goal-line.

For a fixed scrum, the referee should take up his
position near (1) or (1a).   He must see that the
ball is put fairly into the scrum, so it is usual to
stand on the same side as the scrum half.   If the
scrum is near the touch-line and he stands at
position (1a), he may find himself cut off from the
play which follows, so it is preferable to keep on
the side away from the touch-line.   If he *does* stand
at position (1), the referee should look round
occasionally to see that no outside has crept forward beyond the line *AB* before the ball has come
out of the scrum.

For a line-out, it is best to stand at position (2).

A referee can then see that the ball has been thrown over the 5-yards line and he can judge whether it is straight almost as well as if he is at the end of

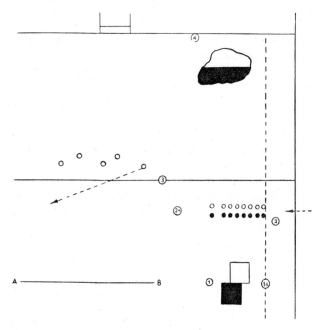

the line. It is a good idea to stand occasionally at position (2a) just to see that there is no charging.

For a drop-out or kick-off, a referee should stand on the line as at (3) so as to be sure that no player crosses the line before the ball is kicked.

When play is near the goal-line, as indicated by the irregular patch on the diagram, it is best for the referee to place himself on the goal-line side of the bunch of players, as at position (4). If the ball is forced over the line, it is essential to see how it got there and not to be unsighted. When the ball is grounded over the line, the referee must try to make a decision that it is either a try or a touch-down; if he cannot make this decision, he should award a 5-yard scrum, giving the defending side the right to put the ball in. It is the vital duty of the referee, therefore, to be on the spot, and this demands a considerable degree of physical fitness. A knowledge of what to do when various contingencies occur in the in-goal area is also important; for this, the study of Laws 18, 30, 31, 32, and 33 is strongly recommended.

Finally, quite apart from all the technical knowledge which he must possess, a good referee should have a considerable amount of tact and a sense of humour which will enable him to see the lighter side of what is, after all, a jolly good game. The responsibility for an enjoyable contest rests very largely on his shoulders, and he—and his whistle—should be as self-effacing as is compatible with the correct interpretation of both the spirit and the letter of the laws of the game.

CHAPTER IX

MODERN TENDENCIES

A. General Organisation

As we have seen, Rugby Football really began in 1823 on the playing-fields of Rugby School; and since Rugby was at that time the pattern for the newer Public Schools, the game spread rapidly from them to the universities of Oxford and Cambridge, and then gradually to the rest of the country. The modern tendency is for this process to continue, for the great game to spread and go on spreading. Some of the finest Rugger in the country is still played at the Public Schools and Universities, but an ever-growing number of boys in the secondary modern schools are learning the game; the result is that in the average club to-day, particularly outside London, men and boys from all walks of life mingle in the happy equality of the fifteen.

The Rugby Union does all it can to help this expansion. The game is becoming better organised, more and more efficient referees are becoming available, and there is a network of voluntary agents covering most of the country on the look-out for good players. The ladder from the humblest club team via the county sides to an England XV is being slowly built up; no potentially great stand-off half need now be born to blush

unseen! The local representative of the Rugby
Union will soon have him in a County Trial and
on the road to fame. Moreover, the Rugby Union
gives financial help to clubs which want to purchase
their own grounds.

But if Rugger is spreading and being better
organised, it is not being commercialised. In an
age of professional sport, the game remains one
which people play because they like playing it, and
its amateur status is jealously guarded. All attempts
to introduce a League, with promotion and relega-
tion, are rightly opposed, for the game would lose
its character as a friendly tussle between fellows
with an afternoon off, and become instead a grim
duel in which those little chats you have with your
opponent in the line-out—and whose nose you hope
shortly to rub in the mud!—would be no more.

In one respect there is perhaps a modern tendency
to overdo organisation from the top. There has
been much criticism lately of the overweighted
programme of county and international matches,
particularly when to these are added foreign and
Dominions' tours. In some seasons during recent
years, the first-class clubs have found the occasions
all too frequent when they could not field their
best sides because their finest players were engaged
in representative matches elsewhere.

B. The Game Itself

So much for modern tendencies in organisation.
What is happening to the game itself? In general,

the most important modern tendency—and the one which is most discussed—is the increasing domination of the play by back-row forwards in defence. Older enthusiasts look back longingly to the golden age of Rugby, before the 1914–18 War, when the indiscriminate hurly-burly was replaced by the passing game in which the forwards scrummaged and took but little part in the open play, while the outsides, unhampered by marauding forwards, fought out their duels in the open. After 1918, forwards took more and more part in open play, so that the three-quarters were forced to rely on opportunism, punting ahead, and kicking for touch. Wing forwards, breaking quickly from the scrum, smothered many an attack before it was begun; and new defence moves tipped the balance against attack, at any rate in international games. In the internationals of the 1948–49 season, for instance, each side averaged only seven points per match.

This development of defensive play by wing forwards has had another effect. Referees, becoming more and more efficient through tests and schemes for training, have become stricter on the off-side law in an effort to check the marauding wing forward. This has added enormously to the number of penalty-kicks awarded, and a very large proportion of games is now decided by the points won from successful penalty-kicks. A side can obtain three easy points as a result of an opponent's infringement near his own goal-posts, yet only three perhaps from a fine piece of combined attacking play which results in a thrilling try near the corner-flag.

This modern tendency to spoil the game through too much defensive work by wing forwards and as the result of too many penalty-kicks is viewed with growing concern by lovers of Rugby, and various remedies have been suggested and tried. One school of thought despairs of curing the evil by legislation, and sees the only hope in training the young on the old ideas. Yet this is hardly practicable; it is no use training some players to adopt the old tactics when forwards were forwards and backs were backs, for as soon as they meet a team playing the modern game, they would be at a grave disadvantage.

In the 1946–47 season, the Rugby Union experimented with a new law in a game between United Services Portsmouth and Richmond. In that match a wing forward was not allowed to break until the ball was clear of the scrum. The result was a fast, open game which the Services narrowly won after more than 50 points had been scored! That shows the result of restricting defensive forward play. Yet in some respects the experiment was inconclusive; the players were aware that it *was* an experiment, and the wing forwards were on their very best behaviour, so much so that there was only one infringement of the new rule. No doubt if the idea were adopted, ways would soon be found to circumvent it. One wing forward, for example, might be taken completely out of the scrum and stationed as an extra defender opposite the stand-off half.

Another remedy—many people think the only one—has been adopted by the Rugby League, the organisation which runs professional Rugby in the north of England, parts of Wales, France, Australia, and New Zealand. There the wing forwards are simply abolished, and there are only six forwards packing 3–2–1. It may be objected that such a reduction in numbers would make the game too fast; it might suit professionals, but Saturday-afternoon players would find it too exhausting. Yet it is difficult to see how any other solution can solve the problem.

To remedy the other defect, the excessive importance of penalty-kicks, there has long been an agitation to reduce their points value to two instead of three. But here again there is a dilemma; if you reduce the value of a free-kick to two points, you reduce the penalty for off-side—and what you gain on the roundabouts you will lose on the swings. One result of all this agitation was the reduction in 1948 of the value of a dropped goal from four points to three. This was probably a good thing in itself, but the penalty-goal, the real villain of the piece, still goes unscathed.

All these problems, and many others, are the concern of the governing bodies of the game; and so long as these bodies continue to keep in intimate touch with clubs, players, and spectators, any future changes will doubtless be for the benefit of the game as a whole.

DVERTISING & PUBLICITY   ALGEBRA   AMATEUR ACTING   ANA

OOK-KEEPING   BRICKWORK   BRINGING UP CHILDREN   BUSINE

CHESS   CHINESE   COMMERCIAL ARITHMETIC   COMMERCIAL AF

COMPOSE MUSIC   CONSTRUCTIONAL DETAILS   CONTRACT BRIDGE

PEEDWORDS   ECONOMIC GEOGRAPHY   ECONOMICS   ELECT

NGLISH GRAMMAR   LITERARY APPRECIATION   ENGLISH RENASC

EVIVAL   VICTORIAN AGE   CONTEMPORARY LITERATURE   ETCH

REELANCE WRITING   FRENCH   FRENCH DICTIONARY   FRENCH

IVING THINGS   GEOLOGY   GEOMETRY   GERMAN   GERMAN

GOOD CONTROL OF INSECT PESTS   GOOD CONTROL OF PLANT DISE

GOOD FARMING BY MACHINE   GOOD FARM WORKMANSHIP   GOO

GOOD MARKET GARDENING   GOOD MILK FARMING   GOOD PIG K

GOOD ENGLISH   GREEK   GREGG SHORTHAND   GUIDEBOOK TO

GREAT BOLIVAR BOTHA   CATHERINE THE GREAT   CHATHAM   CLE

IBERALISM   HENRY V   JOAN OF ARC   JOHN WYCLIFFE   LENIN   LOUIS

ROBES ... HASTING

HOUS ... REPAIRS

WRITE ... ND TO

MECH ... LCRAFT

MOTO ... FICIENC

PHYSI ... DESIG

ADMI ... NG

GIVE INSTRUCTION TO A WISE MAN···

PHR... OOK   SAILING   SALESMANSHIP   SECRETA ... ACTIC

DEBATE ... SPELLING   STAMP COLLECTING   STUDE ... DE

TYPEWRITING   USE OF GEOGRAPHY   WAY TO POETR ... WF

COOKERY FOR GIRLS   DOGS AS PETS FOR BOYS AND GIRLS   KN

PHOTOGRAPHY FOR BOYS AND GIRLS   RADIO FOR BOYS   RIDINC

SOCCER FOR BOYS   STAMP COLLECTING FOR BOYS AND GIRLS   W

ACTING   ANATOMY   ARABIC   ASTRONOMY   BANKING   B

CHILDREN   BUSINESS ORGANISATION   CALCULUS   CANASTA

COMMERCIAL ART   COMMERCIAL CORRESPONDENCE   COMME

CONTRACT BRIDGE   COOKING   CRICKET   DRAWING   DRE

ECONOMICS   ELECTRICITY   ELECTRICITY IN THE HOUSE   ELOC

ENGLISH RENASCENCE   ENGLISH RENASCENCE TO THE ROMANT

LITERATURE   ETCHING   EVERYDAY FRENCH   TO EXPRESS YOU

DICTIONARY   FRENCH PHRASE BOOK   GARDENING   GAS IN

GERMAN   GERMAN DICTIONARY   GERMAN GRAMMAR   GERM

CONTROL OF PLANT DISEASES   GOOD FARM ACCOUNTING

GOOD FARM WORKMANSHIP   GOOD FRUIT FARMING   GOOD G

GOOD MILK FARMING   GOOD PIG KEEPING   GOOD POULTRY K

GREGG SHORTHAND   GUIDEBOOK TO THE BIBLE   HINDUSTANI

CATHERINE THE GREAT   CHATHAM   CLEMENCEAU   CONSTANTINE   C

ARC   JOHN WYCLIFFE   LENIN   LOUIS XIV   MILTON   PERICLES   PETER

USE OF HISTORY   WARREN HASTINGS   WOODROW WILSON   HOC

HOUSEHOLD ELECTRICITY   HOUSE REPAIRS   ITALIAN   JOINEF

MANAGEMENT   MATHEMATICS   HAND TOOLS   ENGINEERIN

DRAUGHTSMANSHIP   METEOROLOGY   MODELCRAFT   MODERN D

MUSIC   NORWEGIAN   PERSONAL EFFICIENCY   PHILOSOPHY   PH

SHORTHAND   PLANNING AND DESIGN   PLUMBING   POLISH